Can I Be in Your Class?

Real Education Reform to Motivate Secondary Students

Can I Be in Your Class?

Real Education Reform to Motivate Secondary Students

Denise Fawcett Facey

ROWMAN & LITTLEFIELD EDUCATION

A division of

ROWMAN & LITTLEFIELD PUBLISHERS, INC.
Lanham • New York • Toronto • Plymouth, UK

Published by Rowman & Littlefield Education
A division of Rowman & Littlefield Publishers, Inc.
A wholly owned subsidary of The Rowman & Littlefield Publishing Group, Inc.
4501 Forbes Boulevard, Suite 200, Lanham, Maryland 20706
http://www.rowmaneducation.com

Estover Road, Plymouth PL6 7PY, United Kingdom

British Library Cataloguing in Publication Information Available

Library of Congress Cataloging-in-Publication Data

Facey, Denise Fawcett, 1958–
  Can I be in your class? : real education reform to motivate secondary students / by
Denise Fawcett Facey.
    p. cm.
  Includes index.
  ISBN 978-1-61048-479-4 (pbk. : alk. paper)—ISBN 978-1-61048-480-0 (electronic)
  1. Education, Secondary—United States.   2. Educational change—United States.
I. Title.
  LA222.F33   2011
373.0973—dc23

                                                                              2011016331

∞ ™ The paper used in this publication meets the minimum requirements of American
National Standard for Information Sciences—Permanence of Paper for Printed Library
Materials, ANSI/NISO Z39.48-1992.

Printed in the United States of America

Contents

Acknowledgments

Although writing tends to be a solitary pursuit, no book is fully accomplished without the help of others. With this in mind, I have several people to thank.

For their invaluable assistance in putting this book together and for their high level of professionalism, I sincerely thank the editorial staff at Rowman and Littlefield Education, particularly Tom Koerner and Lindsey Schauer. Working with them was a pleasure.

My family's belief in me and in my ability to bring this book to fruition spurred me on. I thank my mother and my sister—fellow educators and true cheerleaders in this endeavor—for cheerfully reading the chapters as I wrote them, providing insight into the way educators would respond to the book. And for his boundless enthusiasm for this project, his helpful suggestions, and encouragement, I thank my husband, William.

Finally, to all my students over the years who came in each day eagerly asking, "What are we doing today?" and to every student who stood at my classroom door asking, "Can I be in your class?" I thank you. You were the impetus for this book, the reason teachers teach and the purpose for education reform that makes education meaningful for students.

Collectively, the input of all these individuals is represented in this book, and I am truly grateful to each of you.

Introduction

"I hate school."

"School is boring."

Spoken by countless students, for equally numerous years, the above statements should provoke educators to ask why and to consider the connection between those words and the current state of education in the United States. More often than not, the answer lies not in the content but rather in the uninspiring manner in which teachers convey it, in the emphasis on standardized tests over critical-thinking skills, and in the reliance on oft-repeated methodologies that don't motivate students. Yet, this needn't be the case.

If you stop for a moment and mentally travel back to that time when you were the student instead of the teacher, you may recall the teacher whose class became the one you most enjoyed. Perhaps she taught your favorite subject and made it even more fascinating. Maybe he found a way to enliven your most dreaded course, making you a lifelong fan of it. Or, possibly, this teacher simply provided the nurturing environment in which learning thrived.

Regardless of the reason, those classes excited the students in them and attracted those who were not. Moreover, the sense of anticipation you felt as you entered that classroom each day—the expectation that something good was sure to happen—became an incentive for learning. And genuine, measurable learning did occur in those classrooms. The memory of it all may even elicit a smile today.

Yet, this academically supportive atmosphere has gotten lost amidst today's educational focus on standardized exams and stringent standards for teachers. While standards—for exams and teachers—are a necessary component of educational excellence, successful education reform goes beyond these measures. Therefore, restoring a stimulating and responsive educational environment, and producing successful academic results in the process, are the bases for this book—indeed the bases for real education reform.

For educators seeking authentic reform, it begins in each individual classroom. With this basic concept at the forefront, this book uses sound education principles—rooted in education pioneer John Dewey's theories on experiential learning and psychologist Abraham Maslow's concept of self-actualization— and shapes them in innovative ways to make learning at once attainable, invigorating and fun.

Here you'll learn specific tips and techniques to enhance instruction and pique student interest. From creating a welcoming atmosphere that is conducive to academic exploration to developing lesson plans with real-world connections to devising alternative forms of assessment that gauge genuine learning and progress in your students, this book provides secondary teachers the means to begin education reform in your own classrooms and to make education a wonderful experience. Consider how much more dynamic learning becomes when students actively participate rather than passively absorb.

Designed to enhance and supplement what teachers already do, this book's primary goal is to help teachers enrich students' learning experience while augmenting their academic achievement. The bonus is that it makes teaching a more rewarding experience as well, thereby motivating both students and teacher.

Anecdotes at the start of each chapter reflect real-life situations, while the strategies offered are tools for action that may also generate new methodologies of your own design. Furthermore, the self-assessment worksheets at the end of each chapter, containing ten questions each, help you to personalize and apply the chapter's suggestions. With all this at your disposal, educators who want to facilitate learning as a vibrant, lifelong practice for their students now have the keys to open those educational doors.

So, get ready to begin real education reform, to make learning an action word again, and to include the best practices from that learning environment you fondly recall from your own schooldays. In the process, you'll develop a love of learning in your students. Then you'll have other students eagerly asking, "Can I be in your class?" Far more than a mere stamp of approval, this question conveys students' longing for what you are offering, along with their propensity to work to attain it. That's a foundation for active learning. Let's get started.

Chapter 1

Create a Welcoming Atmosphere

Although Ron had been a high school English teacher for many years, teaching served only as a conduit to his true avocation: football coach. He lived and breathed football, and he considered anything else—including teaching—inconsequential. Never having been the warm and fuzzy type, he had long-established classroom procedures that he maintained specifically because they were expedient. And he never deviated from them.

Not overtly unkind, Ron nevertheless maintained a remote detachment from his students. This clearly meant that cheery greetings and light banter were not part of Ron's parlance—these were alien concepts to him. In fact, quickly learning that a grunt would be the reply to any greetings they offered, his students eventually stopped greeting him.

Ron didn't put a great deal of thought or effort into anything as ordinary as decorating his classroom either. As he saw it, bulletin boards, decorations and the like were unnecessary frivolities having nothing to do with his job. Tacking a couple of football posters to the wall, he figured he had complied with his administrator's edict to prepare his classroom.

Furthermore, since Ron's approach to teaching was equally austere, rather than a class discussion or even a lesson that revolved around a lecture, his students routinely found an assignment awaiting them each day, with accompanying instructions on the board. This procedure enabled Ron to avoid talking to his students, thereby maintaining the distance he preferred. Clearly, activities, projects and the like were unheard of in his classroom.

Instead, upon entering the room, his students quickly fell silent, immediately beginning the assignment, as expected. Submitting their work at the end of the class period, they left the room hurriedly. And throughout the entire

1

time, Ron's only interactions with them were gruff admonitions against talking along with mute directions as to where to place their completed assignments.

So, in much the same way as his students had learned to stop greeting Ron, they also soon realized that if they had any questions, they'd better muddle through rather than risk their teacher's ire by directing their questions toward him. As time went by, not only did the students begin to dread Ron's class, they felt a good deal of animosity toward him as well.

WELCOME STUDENTS

Admittedly an extreme example, Ron is nonetheless not an isolated case. What's worse, to say that his studied indifference caused his students to feel unwelcome in his classroom would be an understatement. And while this may seem insignificant to Ron and teachers like him, from an education standpoint, such an atmosphere proves toxic, inhibiting learning for many students. That's why creating a welcoming atmosphere for students is not a mere nicety but rather an educational imperative. The good news is that it's an easy reform.

Welcoming your students through your words, demeanor, and the atmosphere of your classroom provides the backdrop against which learning more easily begins. While you may not be as reticent toward your students as Ron—that places you a step ahead at the outset—if you're a veteran teacher, you still may want to review your habits to determine whether your students feel genuinely welcome in your classroom. Or if you're just beginning your teaching career, consider what precise steps you might take to make your students feel welcome.

To delve into your mindset about this issue and to determine how welcoming your classroom may be, here are a few questions to ask yourself:

- What specific techniques do I employ to welcome my students?
- Do I greet my students cheerfully, and individually, as they enter my classroom each day?
- What is my general philosophy of education? In other words, do I view education as interactive between the teacher and students as well as among the students? Or does my education philosophy lean more toward students being passive recipients of information? (This is particularly significant, as it will inform your classroom atmosphere.)
- Have I provided an attractive environment in which my students can learn?

- How approachable am I?
- Are students relaxed or tense in my classroom?
- Are my lessons student-focused, as opposed to teacher-focused?

As simplistic or even unnecessary as some of these issues may now seem to you, they are among the important considerations when planning strategies for making your students feel welcome, and by extension, for setting the stage for learning. Furthermore, your responses to these questions, as well as others in the same vein that you may pose yourself, become the first basic step in changing the education paradigm in your classroom—a preliminary move toward bolstering academic progress.

Metaphorically rolling out the welcome mat provides a setting in which students are more likely to engage actively in discovery, discussion and further educational exploration—the qualities that build lifelong learners. Such results are impetus enough for teachers to make a welcoming environment an essential component of the classroom.

GREET YOUR STUDENTS

Let's begin with Ron's first mistake: not greeting his students. Naturally aloof, it probably never occurred to Ron that greetings mattered to high school students. Yet, as innocuous as they may seem, greetings (or the lack thereof) speak volumes about your opinion of your students' importance, even if it is not your intention to convey this sentiment. And your students will surely take note.

Your greeting is the first step in developing a welcoming atmosphere and can set the tone for your class, creating the first impression your students will have of who you are and what your classroom style will be. Therefore, Ron's refusal to address his students became a harbinger of the tense and unyielding environment in which he would expect his students to learn. And his students responded accordingly. That's a difficult setting for academic achievement.

However, Ron could have rectified this aspect of his classroom situation quite easily. Likely to elicit a positive response, which will be reflected in your students' work ethic, a cheerful greeting is akin to waving a magic wand in your classroom; it can transform attitudes and behaviors in a positive way, predisposing students to learning. Thus, the good will engendered by your smile and your friendly greeting extends into your classroom.

This doesn't mean that without a salutation, or with an unpleasant one, students fail to work or learn, but rather that they work with greater enthusiasm and diligence in a pleasant atmosphere, which is what a friendly greeting portends. Simply put, a pleasant greeting motivates students.

Try this simple experiment:

- Stand at your classroom door as your students arrive.
- Greet each student by name as he or she enters.
- Watch the smiles spread across their faces.

By offering a good-humored greeting, you've already connected with your students, and class hasn't even begun yet. Yet, that simple connection can make a profound difference in reaching students.

DECORATE YOUR CLASSROOM

The next step in welcoming your students is via the décor of your classroom. Posh surroundings are not necessary when creating an inviting classroom environment. What matters is that your classroom not appear spare, cold, and unadorned—this reads as unwelcoming to students.

Instead, whether your classroom is in a state of the art building or in an aging edifice, establish a comfortable ambience. In much the same manner as you might cultivate a warm environment in your home for guests, you want to engender a comparable level of warmth in your classroom. Following right behind an amiable greeting, a warm décor comprised of both educational and attractive items, is another preliminary step in easing tension and stress from your classroom.

Serving not only to welcome students, a cheery décor conveys that you value them. After all, you have taken the time to prepare for their arrival. Providing the additional benefit of inspiration and education via décor makes this not just an essential aspect of welcome, but a boon to students' academic progress as well.

And you might be surprised to know that, even unasked, students express a decided preference for classrooms with a cheerful décor over those with bare walls. Since your classroom's décor is such a strong component in creating the warmth that draws students in, here are a few suggestions:

- Display interesting and colorful subject-appropriate posters. Offering visual stimulation, the best aspect of these posters is actually in the academic content students glean from them as they move about the room or as their eyes occasionally wander.
- Uplifting banners and posters provide inspiration and encouragement, making them another excellent selection for classroom display. Easily designed

by printing quotations on large paper, such banners are available ready-made as well, both of which are cheerful decorative elements imparting words of wisdom. Moreover, as you begin the school year, these banners, along with subject-specific posters, are likely to be the only items you have for display. This will soon change as students submit their own work.

- Diversity or multiculturalism is an additional important detail in the selection of posters. Depicting images of people of various ethnicities and races, the inclusion of culturally diverse images is a subtle but significant reflection of your appreciation and respect for students of all backgrounds. This is particularly validating for students whose race or ethnicity is not the majority in the school.
- As the year progresses, students' work—from graded papers to three-dimensional projects—is an excellent addition to classroom walls, bulletin boards and bookshelves. Offering an additional layer of interest to the room, they also bolster students' pride in their own accomplishments, while reflecting your high esteem for their work. Students may never mention it to you, but they appreciate the intrinsic honor.
- Bulletin boards, like posters and banners, provide the perfect backdrop for either content-related items (including students' work) or inspirational matter. If, for example, the bulletin boards pertain only to content, the wall posters and banners might be inspirational, or vice versa. Ensuring that these are colorful and alluring makes them sure to catch your students' eyes. Be sure to continually update them throughout the school year.
- Also, consider photographing your students while they engage in classroom activities. Suspended from the ceiling and/or hung along the walls around your classroom, the photos are a boost to students' self-worth as they see themselves displayed around your classroom. Moreover, knowing that we only display that which we like and admire, this says welcome in a big way.

While not an exhaustive list, the point is to consider strategies for making your classroom décor uniquely yours, yet a place in which your students feel welcome and encouraged. By decorating your room with warmth and attention to educational detail—while ensuring that all adornments are either done by your students or chosen with them in mind—you create a classroom that is reflective of your students and your high regard for them. There's no better way to say welcome.

PROVIDE A RELAXING CLASSROOM ENVIRONMENT

Having provided inviting surroundings, the next consideration in your plan to welcome your students is the atmosphere within those surroundings. It's your next layer of warmth. Ron's aloofness toward his students once they entered his classroom, for example, exacerbated an already tense situation. Therefore, think about the following question: Is my classroom a place where students feel relaxed and comfortable?

This is not a question of formal versus informal nor of strict versus lax. On the contrary, students need to know that there are rules to which they must adhere and consequences when they breach the rules; the absence of rules is not a relaxed atmosphere, but rather anarchy. "Relaxed and comfortable" is a matter of students' sense that your classroom is one in which learning is not an intimidating experience. Thus, the question remains: How relaxed and comfortable do students feel in your classroom?

Consider the fact that from learning to tie their shoes to learning to ride a bike to learning to drive a car, students must acquire myriad skills that are not within the purview of teachers. But if you recall your own learning experiences, you might note that these and many other skills were infinitely easier to learn when done without pressure, raised voices, or tense environments.

If this idea seems immaterial to classroom education, bear in mind that a relaxed environment is more conducive to all types of learning. In view of this, think how much you can facilitate learning when you provide a comfortable atmosphere for your students. After all, making learning easier is part of what teaching is about.

The first step in developing a relaxed classroom environment is to evaluate how well you're already doing on this issue. Once again, ask yourself a few questions:

- How do I speak to my students? Do I often raise my voice or speak sharply?
- How do I respond to students' questions? Am I irritated by the interruption to the pace of my lesson, annoyed by the students' inability to grasp an "easy" concept? Or do I view questions as an opportunity to provide supplementary information, responding accordingly?
- Do I notice when students are struggling or having a bad day? And do I act on what I observe?
- Are students comfortable asking me for help?

You may have other questions that should also be included in this self-assessment; just be sure to give some thought to your classroom's overall atmosphere. Had Ron assessed himself in this manner, he would have found himself wanting. Not only was his classroom environment not easygoing—welcoming students in—his students longed for a way out.

Since it's not difficult to provide a relaxed and welcoming atmosphere in your classroom, here are some tips:

- Make a concerted effort to modulate your voice. Sometimes easier said than done, it pays dividends in terms of reaching your students and creating a tranquil setting. Raising your voice in anger or irritation can become a barrier between you and your students, causing them to shut down, no longer absorbing your lesson.
- Check your tone of voice as well. Words that drip with sarcasm or condescension serve to alienate and hurt students, which definitely is not part of a relaxed environment. Clearly, this will prove counterproductive to your efforts to be an effective teacher.
- Be approachable. Students become tense and apprehensive—and therefore, avoid contact with you—when they believe your response to their questions will be annoyance or derision. Despite the fact that you may not have any objection to their asking questions, unless you make that known to them, some students will prefer bewilderment to venturing a question that could result in your displeasure or their chastisement.
- Be observant. Just as some students never ask questions, others never seek help. Instead, they flounder in confusion, either unaware that they are in need of help or unwilling to seek it. Your vigilance in being alert to students who may be struggling or who just seem a bit perplexed, and then offering your assistance, allows students to find comfort in the knowledge that help is available to them. We'll explore this topic in greater depth in chapter eight.
- Support students in competing with their own past performances rather than with each other. While some students thrive in a competitive milieu, many feel pressured when encouraged to outdo their classmates. On the other hand, students often feel invigorated by their attempts to surpass their own past records. Removing the competitive pressure creates the comfortable environment in which students can then enjoy the challenge of surpassing themselves.

Providing an environment conducive to the give and take of learning, simple adjustments such as these help students to feel comfortable, relaxed and welcome. Furthermore, the ease of incorporating these methods into your daily routine makes this a seamless reform.

DEVELOP A STUDENT-CENTERED CLASSROOM

The next consideration in your quest to welcome your students is what, or better yet, who becomes the central focus of your classroom. Without placing them on a pedestal or giving them control of the classroom, let's make students that focus.

The proviso here is that you not permit a transition to student-centered teaching to become another self-esteem venture. Having put a good deal of emphasis on nurturing students' self-esteem over the last couple of decades, many educators and parents have falsely imbued students with a sense of entitlement that encourages students to believe that high grades are due them rather than earned through their own intense efforts. Therefore, although developing student-centered classrooms is part of the basic premise and overall philosophy for everything in this book, fostering another self-esteem program is not.

In short, for the purposes of this book, the goal of a student-centered classroom is to develop an environment in which the educational needs of the students are paramount. Such an environment tends to augment students' self-concept, but the goal is education. And as trendy as this ideology sounds, it unquestionably promotes learning as it shifts the focus from what is perhaps easiest or most familiar for the teacher to what is most beneficial for the students.

What does a student-centered classroom entail? Among other things, it may include the following:

- Revamping your much-loved lesson plans to make them more participatory for students
- Developing or researching new activities and projects that more readily engage student interest and action
- Considering a style of teaching that is less teacher-dominated. Lessons based solely on students' listening and taking notes are actually teacher-centered, not student centered.
- Reevaluating your educational philosophy such that it is more inclusive of students' learning styles
- Soliciting students' ideas and input in specific educational areas
- Interacting with your students in a manner that encourages dialogue, inquiry, and discovery

In essence, students' needs become the motivating factor for all your classroom endeavors. This necessitates your commitment to evaluating every lesson plan, project, class activity, and interaction between yourself and your students in light of its focus on students. Whenever this central focus shifts, readjust or discard. At times more labor-intensive for you as the teacher— although it becomes less so with practice—the results will be worth the effort: enthusiastic, engaged student participation and authentic student learning.

One caveat: student-centered does not mean student-ruled. As we touched on in our discussion of relaxed classroom environments, it's crucial that you never relinquish your authority in favor of students setting the agenda, and by extension, the rules. The ensuing mayhem would undermine all your educational efforts and inhibit learning. Instead, student-centered is still teacher-ruled; it's a rather benevolent dictatorship.

Clearly, welcoming your students is a combination of many factors. Forming a loose framework within which you can add or change components as you determine to be best suited to your students, you can start the small changes that will make your classroom into a warm and vibrant setting that promotes your students' educational growth and development. In a welcoming classroom, students have the best opportunity to thrive. That's an auspicious beginning!

Chapter One: Create a Welcoming Atmosphere   **Worksheet**

1. How do I know whether students feel welcome in my classroom?

_____

_____

_____

_____

_____

_____

_____

_____

_____

_____

_____

_____

2. What specific techniques will I now use to create a welcoming atmosphere?

_____

_____

_____

_____

_____

_____

_____

_____

_____

_____

_____

_____

_____

Chapter One: Create a Welcoming Atmosphere   **Worksheet**

3. How does my general philosophy of education influence my classroom
   environment?

_____

_____

_____

_____

_____

_____

_____

_____

_____

_____

_____

4. How do I respond to students' questions?

_____

_____

_____

_____

_____

_____

_____

_____

_____

_____

_____

_____

_____

Chapter One: Create a Welcoming Atmosphere **Worksheet**

5. What will I do to make students comfortable asking me for help?

_____

_____

_____

_____

_____

_____

_____

_____

_____

_____

_____

6. How can I make my lessons student-centered?

_____

_____

_____

_____

_____

_____

_____

_____

_____

_____

_____

_____

_____

Chapter One: Create a Welcoming Atmosphere   **Worksheet**

7. What changes in my demeanor would make students more relaxed?

_____

_____

_____

_____

_____

_____

_____

_____

_____

_____

_____

_____

8. What was the result of the greeting experiment in my classroom?

_____

_____

_____

_____

_____

_____

_____

_____

_____

_____

_____

_____

Chapter One: Create a Welcoming Atmosphere   **Worksheet**

9. What suggestions in this chapter will I employ in my classroom?

_____

_____

_____

_____

_____

_____

_____

_____

_____

_____

_____

_____

_____

10. What was the result of my implementation of these suggestions?

_____

_____

_____

_____

_____

_____

_____

_____

_____

_____

_____

_____

_____

Chapter 2

Dare to Be Different

Eagerly anticipating her first day of teaching, Jennifer felt as if she were about to burst with excitement as the day approached. A multitude of creative ideas bounced around in her head as she planned for the upcoming school year. Maybe she would begin with a game to acclimate the students to one another. Perhaps, she mused, she would have a weekly study hour with classical music playing in the background; in her research, she had read that music enhanced learning. She might also incorporate skits and other types of role-playing into her lessons.

Bubbling over with inspiration, Jennifer arrived at the middle school with a mixture of enthusiasm and anxiety. As much as she looked forward to embarking on this fresh venture, she was a bit nervous about undertaking her new responsibilities on her own. So, she mingled with the other teachers that first morning, introducing herself and chatting amicably as she became acquainted with others and relaxed into her new environment.

Casually mentioning some of her plans, Jennifer was surprised when her ideas met with skepticism and even somewhat derisive laughter. "You really are a new teacher," said a veteran teacher, amid collective chuckles from bystanders. A bit taken aback, Jennifer pressed for details about the laughter. Immediately, she was peppered with retorts that stung with each word.

"You can't do that; if you start with games, your class will get out of control and they'll never calm down."

"That's right! Then they'll want to play games every day. You better forget that idea."

"Classical music? The kids will never go for that!"

"Why don't you stop trying to reinvent the wheel and just give them work-sheets when you're not teaching? That will keep them quiet and in their seats."

Taking in these words, Jennifer began to feel defeated before she had even begun. Surely, these teachers knew how to run a classroom; collectively, they had many decades of experience. But Jennifer wanted to be a different kind of teacher. Now she doubted the wisdom of her plans.

DIFFERENT IS NOT ALWAYS WRONG

What a disheartening experience it is for a new teacher to develop exciting plans only to have them shot down by colleagues. Meaning well, the intention of Jennifer's co-workers was to induct the neophyte into the realities of school life by offering what they deemed to be sage advice. However, gradually having lost some of their sense of wonder about what teaching could accomplish, their expectations for what they could elicit from their students also had eroded, now replaced by weary resignation. The result was that their perspectives and Jennifer's were markedly different. But this doesn't make Jennifer wrong.

Some teachers resign themselves to the belief that teaching is an "us" against "them" proposition in which the victor is the one still standing at the end of the school year. In this case, as they saw it, Jennifer's colleagues were helping her to remain standing in the face of imminent insurrection from her students. And they sought to achieve this through long-established, sacrosanct methods.

While we can applaud these teachers' willingness to assist a newcomer, their methodology is off the mark. Obviously focused on what they perceived as most important—crowd control—from their perspective, the main objective was to keep the students still and quiet. And they're not entirely wrong; classroom management is an important skill for any teacher to acquire. Without it, teaching cannot occur, which is why it's a topic covered later in this book.

Where Jennifer's co-workers ran off course, however, was in their emphasis on classroom management to the exclusion of innovative teaching practices. A willingness to try new ways of teaching contributes greatly to dynamic education and is a necessary ingredient in education reform. In this case, not only were these teachers unwilling to "think outside the box," they didn't appear aware that they were in a box. And since Jennifer's ideas were different, they threatened the status quo.

But Jennifer was on the right track before her colleagues derailed her. Her inventive ideas and eagerness to implement resourceful plans are precisely what make classrooms come alive. And, contrary to what the other teachers tried to instill in her, teachers need not ever surrender their sense of awe about teaching or their joy in doing it.

Creative activities and innovative plans like Jennifer's engage students—so much so that behavior problems become far less common (though not non-existent!). Moreover, as a teacher, your enthusiasm for learning and enjoyment of the process will be contagious, greatly reducing all types of classroom management issues. Therefore, when confronted with colleagues like Jennifer's—and you most certainly will be—don't be deterred. Progress with your plans and dare to be different.

This is not different merely for the sake of being so, but rather for the purpose of bolstering education and making it a pleasant process. So, in addition to Jennifer's ideas, here are some others to consider:

- Differentiate your lessons to bolster creativity and to accommodate various learning styles.
- Support active learning
- Make learning experiential
- Arrange creative classroom seating
- Let your students become teachers
- Always remember your own school days

The reasoning behind each of these suggestions may not be readily apparent, but it will be shortly as the explanation of them unfolds. Therefore, consider how you might adapt these tips to your own classroom.

DIFFERENTIATION . . . AGAIN!

While Jennifer's colleagues might well counsel you against innovation, you can give full expression to your creativity—and significantly enhance your students' learning—by differentiating your lessons. A favored educational buzzword of recent years, the word "differentiation" may cause you to shudder at the mere utterance of the word. But take heart—this is a rare instance when, to mangle a cliché, it's as easily done as said.

The core concept of differentiated education is to design curricula and lessons to suit the learning styles and learning needs of your individual students. While this may initially sound rather arduous, developing a different lesson for each student is not entailed. Rather it's a matter of including activities and modifying lessons to heighten learning for everyone. In fact, differentiation lends itself to engaging, imaginative means of learning for students and inventiveness for the teacher.

As a result, you now have a synergistic environment for participation, discovery and further exploration. In short, you have active learning taking place in your classroom. To achieve this through differentiated lesson planning, consider the following:

- Vary your use of activities to include motivating, building, and culminating activities. Motivational activities, for example, that require student involvement—from kinesthetic activities to discussions—spark student interest in the lesson being introduced. Building activities, on the other hand, reinforcing concepts previously taught, link new concepts with those already presented. And culminating activities sum up all that has been learned. Therefore, all of these activities appeal to auditory, kinesthetic, and visual learners.
- Incorporate diversity into your curriculum. Meeting the educational needs of all students, not just those of specific subgroups, the inclusion of the contributions of people from various ethnic groups, races, and abilities (or disabilities) adds interest and depth while simultaneously broadening students' concepts of who these groups are, often redefining them in a positive way in the process. Every academic domain from English to social studies to science to the fine arts lends itself to this inclusion of multicultural contributions and advances as part of the regular course of study, not as a separate celebration. This type of differentiation fits learning needs as well as all learning styles.
- Integrate small-group projects or paired activities into your lessons. Requiring students' combined efforts, while providing opportunities for shared thoughts and ideas, these activities are especially compatible with auditory and kinesthetic learners.
- Devise period-long review sessions as "challenges." Helpful for all types of learners, these challenges reinforce concepts and are especially useful in preparation for exams. For instance, you might divide the class into two teams (and, if desired, team members may create team names). Competing to earn points by correctly answering questions posed by the teacher, the first team to earn ten points wins. These points might then be added to their next test grade or used in another educationally appropriate manner.
- Use various forms of technology in your lessons. Ubiquitous, therefore essential for students amidst global competition, technology enlivens learning and is suitable to all learning styles. Moreover, it can be instrumental in accommodating the needs of students with learning disabilities, whether in a special education class or not. For example, computers, already imperative for all students' research and reports, also augment note taking for

students with disabilities in written expression. For students with visual impairments, the audio component now included in the most popular word processing program is especially beneficial. And the sheer enjoyment students derive from lessons integrated with interactive white boards, laptops, online educational games and the like, make education fun.

- Debates in which students are required to defend the position with which they disagree sharpen critical-thinking skills while simultaneously appealing to auditory and kinesthetic learners.
- Role-playing historic events or literary works is an enjoyable way to provide verbal, visual, auditory and kinesthetic reinforcement of content for students, meeting not only students' learning styles, but also their learning needs.
- Class discussions that link content information with current issues make the content more relevant to students' lives and increase learning. For verbal and auditory learners, this type of activity is especially useful.

These are but a few of the limitless means to differentiate your lessons, supporting all students' learning styles and learning needs, while also kindling student interest and participation. Devising innovative lessons becomes easier and more enjoyable over time, and the students' response to your efforts is even more gratifying. Plus, your creativity gets a boost in the process.

SUPPORT ACTIVE LEARNING

Differentiated learning almost automatically entails active learning as opposed to passive. Participatory in nature, active learning encourages students to go beyond the basics of simply reading the text and answering questions at the end of a chapter or listening to a lecture and taking notes, both of which are common forms of passive learning. Instead, like the types of activities listed in the last segment, active learning lends itself to student involvement, even immersion, in their acquisition of knowledge.

The clear advantages of active learning over passive are numerous and are what make this type of learning a difference worth incorporating. Its advantages include:

- Students retain more information. Acquired through students' own efforts—even if facilitated by the teacher—active learning is more memorable, enabling students to retain more content.
- Active learning more often engages the students' critical-thinking skills. Although reading, for example, necessitates an expenditure of time and a

modicum of effort, and note taking requires students' attention, neither of these requires a good deal of higher-order thinking. Active learning does.

- Students' creativity is developed. Frequently eliciting students' opinions, ideas, handiwork and other input, active learning assists students in synthesizing information to become more inventive and original.
- Classroom management is enhanced. Actively engaged in learning and in working with classmates, students focus on the task before them and are less likely to present behavioral problems in the classroom.
- Students undertake responsibility for their own education. No longer able to cast blame on teachers for boredom or incomprehension, or on parents for not assisting them or simply on adverse circumstances that may arise, students participating in active learning are collaborators with the teacher in producing their own learning.
- Active learning promotes a strong work ethic. Success in these types of tasks requires students' full engagement, putting forth energy and effort not usually dispensed in passive types of learning.
- Students enjoy learning. As is emphasized throughout this book, the enjoyment of learning is integral to sustained achievement. Actively participating in their own learning, students savor the process. And that's the point here.

MAKE LEARNING EXPERIENTIAL

Teachers like Jennifer's co-workers, mentioned at the beginning of this chapter, usually think of teaching as an endeavor best done in classrooms. Given time, they can probably develop an extensive list of grim situations that will befall the teacher who steps beyond those four walls. However, doing so is yet another opportunity to shake up a humdrum atmosphere and dare to be different.

While the usual lessons that entail a teacher writing on a board and students taking notes generally do occur indoors, it's refreshing to incorporate other venues, adding dimension to education by making learning experiential. Whether you remain on campus, traverse the neighborhood, venture into a nearby city or jet off to locales that are more exotic, you broaden your students' information base and make book knowledge more tangible by leaving your classroom.

Among the numerous options to include might be the following:

- Simply taking your role-playing activities to the campus lawn, gives you far more space and removes the need to contain the noise that accompanies such activities. Working equally well for lessons that are primarily discussion, students enjoy the change of scenery.

- A nature walk with your environmental science or biology students, touring the campus or the adjacent vicinity, and allowing students to identify concepts that they have previously only discussed in class or read in a textbook, provides context for the information.
- Visiting local historic sites that are alluded to in a novel your class is reading or that are highlighted in the portion of history your students are currently studying is another way to remove the walls surrounding your classroom.
- Tourist attractions such as aquariums, planetariums, museums, and the like are often overlooked by native residents (such as your students), but are excellent resources for teachers seeking to expand their classrooms, linking content with real-world examples.
- Local theater productions offer budding thespians (and students who just may not have experienced live theater) a proximal view of actors performing their craft. Effectively tying literature and the arts, reading plays will never be the same again.

More than ordinary field trips, a plethora of interesting opportunities for learning outside of the classroom is available. So, when planning units, be imaginative in designing lessons that use other venues to enrich and enliven learning.

ARRANGE CREATIVE SEATING

In addition to differentiating activities as a springboard for active learning, seating can have a significant impact on learning and student interaction as well. If asked, Jennifer's co-workers would likely instruct her to arrange the desks in her classroom in straight rows, facing the board. After all, this is the way it's been done for more years than anyone can recall. From the inception of one-room classrooms to the dawn of the computer age, most teachers have rigidly adhered to this format.

Yet, the real question is why more teachers don't consider any variations on this arrangement. The likely answer is that it's familiar and, therefore, comfortable. Step out of that comfortable niche and try something different.

The best seating plan for your classroom is contingent upon the activities that will take place there. Therefore, as you contemplate the various undertakings that you might introduce in your classroom, let those pursuits guide you in devising your seating plan. Think seriously, about what most supports your goals, and then implement that arrangement. For example:

- Perhaps most conducive to debates and role-play is a semi-circle that allows students to have an unobstructed view of all speakers.

- On the other hand, maybe a large rectangular formation, in which the corners remain open to aid egress, is best if students will often move about for group work. This arrangement also once again enables students to see one another clearly.
- Additionally, consider several long tables rather than individual desks if you frequently include group work or experiments in your lesson plans. This will provide ready-made groups that you can easily change as desired.
- Maybe reconfiguring seating to accommodate specific projects and lessons each time you undertake a new one will work best in your classroom.

The point is that you not immediately conform to the traditional type of arrangement simply because it is the tradition. Moreover, these different types of seating configurations afford teachers a better view of all students, thereby preventing off-task activities. Consider the arrangement most favorable to the sort of lessons you plan to conduct, and position the seating accordingly.

STUDENTS CAN BE TEACHERS

As unorthodox—and, therefore, shocking—as it would seem to teachers who eschew change and cling to formality, allowing your students to become teachers occasionally is a worthwhile variation. As teachers, students directly instruct the class in their own pertinent areas of expertise.

Not as ridiculous as it initially sounds, students discover several educational truths, among which are:

- Students have skills that others (including you) may lack. Enthralled by the mere discovery of this fact, students then feel empowered by your invitation to share their knowledge. To retain the ensuing admiration from peers, they will work hard to ensure the accuracy of their presentation, once again sharpening their work ethic.
- Students hone their public speaking skills as well as their ability to convey their knowledge to others. A true case of practice makes perfect, standing before their classmates is an intimidating task that becomes easier and better done by repetition.
- Students gain a different perspective on how learning occurs. Now on the other side of the teacher's desk, students begin to realize the intricacies of explaining concepts and making them understood. Their newfound appreciation for the demands of teaching encourages them to be more supportive of teachers' attempts to convey information.

- Students can then bolster their own learning. Experiencing learning from a teaching perspective, students soon discover that in order to teach, one must first thoroughly learn the topic. And, not wanting to endure the mocking of peers, they will certainly arrive well prepared to instruct.

Permitting students the privilege to instruct their classmates—and presenting it as such—you assert your confidence in them, causing them to rise to the occasion. Moreover, students' sense of accomplishment resulting from this endeavor is priceless.

Granted, initially you may feel uneasy about allowing students to encroach upon your territory. That's understandable. Believing that you lack both the time and the inclination to cede power to students, your immediate reaction may be to dismiss this as a frivolous notion, despite the benefits students may accrue. In that case, entertain the idea as an educational experiment and analyze the outcome. If you find the results favorable, you'll know your experiment merits repetition.

To get the process started, here are some painless ways to let your students shine:

- When some students remain perplexed despite your repeated explanation of a lesson or concept, ask a volunteer to explain it to the class. Students' presentation of the information in their own unique way can suddenly bring understanding to the formerly bewildered. Everyone involved gains from this experience.
- Students often have technological skills that exceed those of their teachers. Presented a perfect opportunity to teach you or to assist you when technical troubles arise, these same students also are great teaching assistants, guiding less-adept classmates through a lesson that uses technology.
- Dividing a unit or chapter into portions assigned to groups of students allows each group to become the expert on its portion, and subsequently, to teach the class about it.
- Requiring each student to present a research project in class necessitates that each explain (i.e. teach) his or her findings to the class as well.

The successful results from implementation of any of these suggestions will dispel any disquieting feelings you may experience. In fact, after trying it once, chances are high that having students as teachers will become a recurrent practice in your classroom.

The bonus is that students enjoy the opportunity to display their skills and talents. By allowing them to become the teacher, you afford them that chance, while simultaneously boosting their confidence. You're daring to be different.

REMEMBER THE BEST OF YOUR OWN SCHOOL DAYS

One of the finest methods for creating a distinctive classroom—one that is distinguished by its positive attributes—is to recall your own days as a student. Different form the earlier recollection of treasured school-time memories in the introduction of this book, the focus now is on aspects of your own education that you *disliked* back then. For these often are the most effective motivators of change in your own classroom today.

So, recall the class you abhorred, the teachers whose methods you dreaded, the projects you disdained as meaningless. Tenaciously clung to by some teachers, these boring, yet deeply entrenched methodologies that you disliked as a student live on in some of today's classrooms. Now, with the exception of homework and tests—even these need not be the tedious chores you remember—banish them from your present classroom forever.

The fact is, whatever you found repugnant as a student, is just as objectionable to your own students, and is usually unnecessary to inflict on them. Some such offenses include:

- Worksheets that are simply repetitions of the textbook, in addition to being tedious, don't advance or enhance your lessons. Reason enough to forego their use, relegate these to your sub-folder, for distribution in your absence.
- Reliance on the same overhead sheets and/or power point presentations year after year is unimaginative and, eventually, outdated. Refine, update, and edit these on a regular basis to keep your lessons fresh and interesting.
- Lessons in which students read the chapter, answer the questions at the end and then write definitions for the vocabulary, without any additional input from the teacher, are boring and archaic. Not actually representative of teaching, which by definition requires interaction between student and teacher, if you must assign such work, do so for homework.
- Lessons comprised solely of the teacher lecturing for the entire class period and students taking notes may occur from time to time, but should not be a daily occurrence. Interspersing the lecture with discussion, activities, movies, or other enhancements makes for a more vibrant lesson.
- Assigning homework just for the sake of it is meaningless. Not mere busy work to be done at home, homework should have a specific purpose. Fewer but more in-depth assignments may result, which is preferable, as it is a more educational experience for students.

• Developing tests whose answers require only rote memorization not only inhibits the development of critical-thinking skills (which are essential in higher education and in later employment), but it also prohibits students from conveying the full extent of their knowledge.

This list, albeit limited, is also somewhat subjective. Taking the time to give a bit of thought to the transformative techniques that you might employ, edit your lesson plans accordingly, as you dare to make your class different.

Chapter Two: Dare to be Different   **Worksheet**

1. What new activities (motivational, building, or culminating) can I introduce to infuse my lessons with more interest?

   _____

   _____

   _____

   _____

   _____

   _____

   _____

   _____

   _____

   _____

   _____

   _____

   _____

2. How can I integrate technology into my lessons more often?

   _____

   _____

   _____

   _____

   _____

   _____

   _____

   _____

   _____

   _____

   _____

   _____

Chapter Two: Dare to be Different **Worksheet**

3. How can I make the seating in my classroom more conducive to learning?

_____

_____

_____

_____

_____

_____

_____

_____

_____

_____

_____

_____

_____

4. How can I extend my classroom to the surrounding campus?

_____

_____

_____

_____

_____

_____

_____

_____

_____

_____

_____

_____

_____

Chapter Two: Dare to be Different   **Worksheet**

5. How can I make my town and nearby cities part of my lesson plans?

_____

_____

_____

_____

_____

_____

_____

_____

_____

_____

_____

_____

_____

6. When can I let my students become the teachers?

_____

_____

_____

_____

_____

_____

_____

_____

_____

_____

_____

_____

_____

_____

Chapter Two: Dare to be Different **Worksheet**

7. What aspects of my teaching represent status quo methods that need revision?

_____

_____

_____

_____

_____

_____

_____

_____

_____

_____

_____

_____

8. How can I revamp tests to make them a more accurate gauge of students' knowledge?

_____

_____

_____

_____

_____

_____

_____

_____

_____

_____

_____

_____

Chapter Two: Dare to be Different **Worksheet**

9. What other suggestions in this chapter will I employ in my classroom?

_____

_____

_____

_____

_____

_____

_____

_____

_____

_____

_____

_____

_____

10. What was the result of my implementation of these suggestions?

_____

_____

_____

_____

_____

_____

_____

_____

_____

_____

_____

_____

_____

Chapter 3

Defuse the Power of Tests

Biology, chemistry, environmental science—in all its forms, science was Jason's idea of a good time. And teaching eighth grade was equally exciting. He loved conducting experiments that made his students' hair literally stand on end, enabled pumpkins to float, or kept eggs intact while being dropped. Captivating his students with the various roles science played in their daily lives, he continually fueled his own passion for the subject.

However, with the need to meet federal standards, administrators in Jason's school district developed a sense of urgency regarding standardized exam scores, causing them gradually to mandate changes in teaching methods. Bit by bit, like many other teachers, Jason felt compelled to forego experiments and other engaging activities for a greater emphasis on test preparation.

Averse to "teaching to the test," he was reluctant to surrender his own teaching methods. Yet, as he saw it, he had precious little time left to continue the lively, hands-on lessons that he and his students enjoyed. Jason felt as if he were on a treadmill, running in place, as he tried to keep pace with the demands on him and still fulfill his own desire for innovation—and innovation seemed to be losing.

Instead, Jason administered practice tests and review tests, and of course, his own unit tests that determined students' knowledge of what he had taught. In short, standardized test preparation ruled the day. For his students, the joys of discovering science gave way to the drudgery of concentration on exams, and class became far less appealing.

Aware of this, what Jason wanted most was to find a way to do it all. He just wasn't sure how to accomplish this.

TEACHING IN THE REAL WORLD

Jason's dilemma is common. In fact, if you've been teaching for even a brief period, you may find his situation quite familiar. Torn between his desire to immerse his students in the attention-grabbing realm of science and his district's mandate that standardized tests become the central focus in classrooms, Jason is frustrated. Actually, his predicament is perhaps where education reform is most needed.

Granted, you have a limited time allotment in which to convey information, prepare students for exams and try to make the whole process interesting. Juggling so many priorities often means that the teacher—perhaps inadvertently—drops at least one along the way. Possibly inserting an appealing lesson here or a fascinating project there seems remote at best.

However, the fact is that standardized test scores hold great sway in our current educational climate and their preeminence shows no sign of abating any time soon. Actually, although it's debatable, many consider test scores the best indicator of educational excellence. And it's this mindset that places mounting pressure on teachers to produce high scores. Thus, while education leaders may continue to debate the merits of this current educational trend, you must contend with what is. And real-world solutions are what you need.

That solution begins with working within the dictates of our test-conscious education world to make learning enticing for your students, while also producing measurably successful test results. It's vital to your students' education that you integrate educational mandates with educational creativity. In so doing, you offer your students education that is relevant, accessible and enjoyable—while achieving the mandated standards. Here are some practical considerations that can help you achieve these objectives and gain a fresh perspective on them:

- Prioritize your lessons' components
- Redirect your students' focus
- Use alternate means of assessment
- Allow your students to assess you
- Refine your tests
- Rethink grade calculations
- Use data as a teaching tool

As we expound upon these ideas in this chapter, consider the overall goals of your district's mandates and ways to merge them with these suggestions. Using these goals as a guideline, personalize them for your own students so that you meet mandates while infusing your lessons with ingenuity and inspiration. Yes, Jason, it is possible to have it all.

PRIORITIZE YOUR LESSONS' COMPONENTS

Lessons, unit tests, standardized tests, projects, fairs, experiments—all of these vie for equal time in your lesson planning. The dilemma is to harmonize these components such that the time devoted to each upholds your overall goals and objectives. Additionally, of course, you would like to avoid inflicting the boredom that besets so many students compelled to sit through tedious periods of test-centered lessons. You are contending with quite a bit, to say the least.

This is where prioritizing becomes not merely helpful but essential. From a strictly educational point of view, the top priority for classroom teachers is to convey information in a manner that their students comprehend and retain. Furthermore, for teachers seeking to reach beyond standardized tests to stimulate thought and spur active learning, doing so is an additional priority. Clearly, ranking these priorities is in order.

First, consider your main concepts and objectives. Adding interesting accents to these basic elements, you are now ready to present it all in an engaging, interactive manner. If this sounds a bit esoteric, when broken down, it is actually not an onerous task. Just be sure to allot sufficient time—a week or two in advance—for lesson preparation. Here's a way to develop your priorities:

- As your initial priority, devise lessons that contain all the basic content your students need to learn, as well as ways to make it easily understood.
- Next, build critical-thinking skills by including questions that require open-ended responses. Founded on comparisons and contrasts, inferences, drawing conclusions, these types of questions provide opportunities for students to apply and synthesize the content learned. Plus, the development of critical-thinking skills bolsters standardized test-taking achievement by requiring students to assess content beyond mere memorization. And the ability to use these skills is another means of assessing students' content knowledge.
- Now it's time to add in the enjoyable elements. Reinforcing concepts, weave in the most engaging portions of your lessons—activities, experiments, projects, and the like. These enrich knowledge while also enlivening learning. In selecting these lesson enhancements from books, web sites, and your own design, also recall our discussion of students as teachers in chapter two, and try including activities conceived by your students as well. Regardless of the source, these additions to lessons make content more memorable.

Combined, these steps assist not just in prioritizing the components of your lessons, but also in creating interesting, participatory lessons that teach content, develop skills, and meet test preparation objectives. Best of all, this requires only a modicum of your effort to achieve a significant and lasting outcome for your students.

REDIRECT YOUR STUDENTS' FOCUS

Like teachers, students experience the pressures of high-stakes exams. Anxiety provoking, these exams can make even capable students so tense at the actual test time that they seem inept and unskilled, negating both the content and the skills they may have acquired. That's why redirecting students' focus—from exams to content and skills—even before exam season arrives, is one of the best ways to defuse the power of these tests.

When confident of their knowledge and skills, students are less likely to find exams intimidating. This significantly reduces test anxiety and increases the likelihood of better achievement. Therefore, while you cannot eliminate the need for your students to take exams—as much as they wish you could—relieving some of the accompanying distress, thereby improving your students' test-taking ability, is within your reach.

Among the methods for focusing students' attention on the content rather than the exams are the following suggestions:

- Refrain from constantly referring to the standardized exams. Relaying their own apprehension to their students by repeatedly raising the issue of exams, teachers inadvertently heighten students' nervousness. Eliminating these continual references, you remove a portion of the angst that students feel in relation to exams. Simply teach your lessons, with exam preparation in mind, but without overt emphasis on it.
- Reinforce the content by layering it. Ensuring that the content is not merely delivered, but also received and retained, convey it in layers that progressively reinforce the information. For example, first explain the content in detail, and then require that your students write the content through note taking, followed by essays and research papers. You might also moderate discussions of the content among the students. And, finally, include hands-on activities and projects. Essentially incorporating the differentiation tips suggested in chapter two, these tactics reinforce the content, making it more interesting and providing greater depth as well.
- Be repetitious. Seemingly counterintuitive, and even sounding a bit monotonous, repetition works not only for reinforcement purposes, but also for the assistance of those students having difficulty grasping the concepts. By various means, such as reviewing the previous day's content at the beginning of the lesson each day, interspersing prior concepts in current

lessons and linking content from one lesson with that in another, repetition elevates the importance of content.

Effectively diminishing the power of exams to affect students adversely, these guidelines help students to focus on content rather than tests. The bonus is that these suggestions also assist your students in absorbing the necessary information. For some students, this is the difference between success and failure.

REFINE YOUR TESTS

Having just discussed the need to deemphasize tests, you won't be surprised to find that you will still need to administer them—a variety of exams, in fact. In addition to standardized tests, teachers administer unit tests, chapter exams, and quizzes. However, teachers generally have no input in the development of standardized exams. To the extent that teachers have decision-making power in the design of other exams administered, they should include a means for students to convey their knowledge in more than one way. This is where you have a good deal of leeway.

Standard procedure often is to use a multiple-choice exam. Not wrong in itself, this type of exam frequently contains only questions requiring definitions or other low-level skills. Instead, think beyond this rudimentary level to come up with more multifaceted exams. Try developing tests that include each of the following:

- Questions formatted to correspond to the type that students will encounter on standardized exams. For example, devise multiple-choice questions that rely on higher-order thinking in addition to identification of specific concepts.
- Questions requiring short answers also fit the bill. Affording students the chance to identify and analyze concepts—providing fuller answers than those permitted by multiple-choice questions—these questions allow students to demonstrate their knowledge fully. Additionally, they reinforce students' understanding of information needed for standardized exams.
- Free response or essay questions compel students to use their writing skills to develop answers that are more complex. Containing the added advantage of enhancing students' writing abilities, this format also offers the best opportunity for students who have difficulty with multiple choice or short answers to demonstrate their knowledge.

The point is to elicit students' knowledge and skills, not to format questions to confound them and hinder their ability to decipher the question. These adjustments will not only support compliance with district mandates for test preparation, they provide the latitude to design tests that are more conducive to student achievement. Thus, interlaced with the other suggested measures, these reforms fortify students' test-taking ability without the relentless reminder of imminent exams or the tedium of drill exercises. Students' collective sigh of relief is almost audible!

USE ALTERNATE MEANS OF ASSESSMENT

Not the only forms of assessment at a teacher's disposal, tests are also not always the best determinant. While proven adequate in measuring knowledge, they sometimes fall short as a means of quantifying application of that knowledge. Furthermore, tests are certainly a poor gauge of creativity, underscoring the need for alternate means of assessment. Therefore, in addition to tests, the inclusion of some of the following assessment techniques is worth consideration:

- Essay questions, not only excellent additions to exams, as mentioned above, are also a superlative choice to replace traditional exams. They require students to expound upon and connect information acquired— rather than simply parrot what they have heard and memorized—allowing them to display their knowledge in an expanded format. Moreover, by wording the questions to command a higher order of thinking than traditional multiple-choice and fill-in questions, you permit students the freedom to digress from one-word answers and to elaborate beyond short answers.
- Research papers, affording students the opportunity for in-depth study of a topic, increase their knowledge base while simultaneously compelling them to explain it in writing. By allowing students to choose an area of interest for their research pursuits (within parameters that you set), you offer an additional benefit that tends to intensify their efforts. A bonus of research papers is their intrinsic value as an assessment of students' ability to extract new information and collate it with that learned in class.
- Projects, prolific in their versatility, are among the best assessment tools available to teachers. Assigned on a monthly or quarterly basis or just one per semester, they are excellent as culminating activities for a chapter, a unit or a semester. Alternatively, as a year-long endeavor, students conduct research on an ongoing basis, developing a synthesis of that year's education. Providing students both an educational and creative outlet, projects equip teachers with a tool to assess content knowledge and creativity along with students' ability to analyze and compile information.

- Small-group activities that generate collaborative products and independent activities rendering singular products provide more assessment opportunities. Presentations—audio, written reports, Power Points—as well as student-created DVDs, photo essays, and the like exemplify this category of assessment devices. Providing students a divergent learning path, they permit teachers to focus on specific concepts and skills, then evaluate students' grasp of them by their ability to complete the activity successfully.

Each type of assessment helps teachers discern whether their students have learned the requisite information and skills, and to appraise students' ability to use these concepts effectively. Not only is the goal of eliminating the emphasis on tests accomplished, most rewarding is the fact that your students will enjoy learning, while unwittingly preparing for standardized exams. And you can use these suggestions as springboards to creative assessments that you devise.

ALLOW STUDENTS TO ASSESS YOUR WORK

Fully aware of the necessity and benefits of appraising students, educators don't usually consider the value of allowing students to turn the tables. Yet, evaluation of teachers yields important information—and not only when done by administrators. In much the same way as teachers, as practitioners on the frontlines of education, are a valuable—and often overlooked—resource in analyzing the changes needed for education reform, students are a great untapped resource in providing vital information on whether teachers' methods and reforms are achieving their desired goals.

Injecting your lessons with new ideas and practices is initially an experimental endeavor, often fraught with uncertainty regarding its ongoing success. By allowing your students to assess your new undertakings and your overall approach, you equip yourself with a reasonably accurate gauge of what works well with them and what does not.

Toward that end, here are a few useful techniques:

- Develop a list of open-ended questions to distribute to your students after the completion of new activities. Designed uniquely for each activity, the questions enable students to critique the components of the activity and to offer suggestions as well. Of course, their responses are anonymous to encourage complete honesty.
- A response box is another means of obtaining feedback from students. Placing one in an easily accessible location, but not in your usual line

of vision, affords students the opportunity to express their reactions to ongoing methodologies, activities and changes (e.g. the validity of such changes as seating arrangements). This practice is particularly conducive to modifying your reforms in a timely manner.

- Design an evaluation form much like those distributed at the conclusion of a college course. To be completed by your students at the end of each semester, this form might include both multiple choice and free response questions that cover everything from methods to activities and projects to classroom décor to your level of responsiveness to their individual needs. An area for additional comments allots students a chance to provide information that you might not have thought to ask, but which, nonetheless proves advantageous as you continue to refine your practices.

Given the respect of valuing their opinions, students appreciate the opportunity to participate in making their own education as beneficial as possible. Moreover, as participants rather than spectators, they have a vested interest in the realization of an energized educational atmosphere that produces enjoyable learning. Everyone wins!

RETHINK GRADE CALCULATIONS

When calculating their students averages for report card purposes, many teachers give greater weight to exams than to any other assessment. The basis for this decision tends to be a combination of tradition and the belief that exams are more important than any other assessment tool. It's time to rethink this belief.

Among the sound arguments against counting exams more heavily than other grades are the following:

- Doing so gives exams inordinate power. Taking on an inflated importance, one test can conceivably alter a grade point average by a full letter grade, weakening the cumulative effect of students' other grades.
- Students' test anxiety is exacerbated. Aware of the significance of test grades, students' already existing anxiety about tests rises.
- It defeats the purpose of refocusing students' attention from exams. Attempts to redirect student attention to content and skills are thwarted by weighting test grades.
- It undermines the significance of other assignments. All other assignments, from class work to homework to projects, pale in comparison and are likely to receive less effort as a result.

Instead, think outside the usual constraints for a moment. If you have accepted the premise that other assessments (and the assignments they represent) are equally important for gauging students' knowledge, it stands to reason that you would make these alternate assessments equally important when calculating grades. Consider using one of the following options or a combination thereof:

• Weight all assignments (including tests) equitably. This takes the onus off one specific assessment tool and bestows equal credibility on all of them.
• Calculate grades for projects more heavily. Requiring more time and research lends credence to the idea of counting projects more heavily than tests or any other assessment, if one type is to be given more weight. This method also encourages students to see a correlation between their time expenditure and the grade earned for the assignment.
• Count tests more heavily than class work and homework, but not as heavily as projects, if you want to portray tests as being of greater significance than regular assignments. For teachers who are squeamish about the idea of counting all assessments equally, this option adjusts the weight of assignments, yet does not exaggerate the importance of exams.

By reassessing the way you calculate grades, you have the chance to tailor their impact in a manner that is academically effective, while adapting your procedures to the best interests of your own students.

USE DATA AS A TEACHING TOOL

In view of your grading system modifications and your implementation of varied assessments, the data resulting from these can be used for your students' benefit. In fact, as a facilitator of learning, evaluative data might be the best teaching tool available.

Far more than a mere end in and of themselves, the combined results of all the various types of assessments you administer are excellent gauges of student's acquisition of knowledge. Used effectively, this information may then guide you in determining students' learning needs, deciding what needs to be taught, or re-taught, as the case may be.

There are several ways that this data can boost learning, such as:

• Pre-tests of a teacher's own design, for instance, are a great means to judge student knowledge at the outset of the semester. Not factored into students' grades point averages—therefore, not another source of students' anxiety—such a test would cover the major topics that the students should already know as well as those that the teacher plans to cover. The questions missed by most students will indicate what you need to cover. Teachers should be sure to inform students that the exam is merely an assessment tool and not part of their overall grade.

- Unit tests can reveal concepts that require reinforcement. For example, test questions on which a predetermined percentage of the class score incorrect answers warrant review of those topics with your students.
- Post-tests provide yet another source of information that is useful for instruction. By readministering the same pre-test at the end of the semester or at the end of the course, the teacher is able to determine the concepts and skills the students have gained in the course.

As a teaching tool, data promotes learning by assisting teachers in differentiating their lessons according to their students' learning needs. Intended to relieve some of the stress attendant to exams (for both teachers and students), the suggestions offered in this chapter also help in meeting the competing demands of genuine teaching and preparing for exams.

The bonus is that your students will recognize your attempts to replace their anxieties with well-conceived preparation tools as a clear indication that you understand their concerns—that you're on their side. That's a motivational tool likely to elicit their wholehearted participation and increased diligence.

Chapter Three: Defuse the Power of Test   **Worksheet**

1. What "real world" issues have been obstacles to my teaching ideals?

_____

_____

_____

_____

_____

_____

_____

_____

_____

_____

_____

2. What specific steps can I take to accommodate district mandates while also achieving my own educational goals?

_____

_____

_____

_____

_____

_____

_____

_____

_____

_____

_____

Chapter Three: Defuse the Power of Tests   **Worksheet**

3. How can I bolster my students' critical-thinking skills?

_____

_____

_____

_____

_____

_____

_____

_____

_____

_____

_____

_____

4. Which upcoming lessons can I enliven with activities, experiments, etc.?

_____

_____

_____

_____

_____

_____

_____

_____

_____

_____

_____

_____

_____

_____

Chapter Three: Defuse the Power of Tests   **Worksheet**

5. What specific steps can I take to shift my students' focus from exams to content?

_____

_____

_____

_____

_____

_____

_____

_____

_____

_____

_____

_____

6. What assessment tools, other than tests, would be useful for my students?

_____

_____

_____

_____

_____

_____

_____

_____

_____

_____

_____

_____

Chapter Three: Defuse the Power of Tests　　　　　　　**Worksheet**

7. How can I change the format of my tests to prepare my students better for standardized exams?

_____

_____

_____

_____

_____

_____

_____

_____

_____

_____

_____

_____

8. How can I change the way I currently calculate grades to enhance student achievement?

_____

_____

_____

_____

_____

_____

_____

_____

_____

_____

_____

_____

Chapter Three: Defuse the Power of Tests   **Worksheet**

9. What other suggestions in this chapter will I employ in my classroom?

_____

_____

_____

_____

_____

_____

_____

_____

_____

_____

_____

10. What was the result of my implementation of these suggestions?

_____

_____

_____

_____

_____

_____

_____

_____

_____

_____

_____

_____

_____

Chapter 4

Connect the Dots

"Why do we have to learn this?" asked a plaintive voice from the back of the room.

Kristen was as weary of hearing this question as she was of the complaining note in her student's voice. But she refrained from the petulant response that sprang to mind. "Math is an important subject," she replied, "You'll need it for almost anything you want to be in life." Still, she felt frustrated by the repeated need to defend her coursework.

She knew that mathematical concepts weren't the most scintillating topic for her ninth-grade students. But since understanding math was essential not only for school but for life, she didn't see why her students balked at learning it. Besides, in Kristen's opinion, math could be intriguing if they gave it a chance.

Much like solving a mystery or putting together a difficult puzzle, to Kristen, there was a sense of accomplishment in figuring out the right answer. This was what she loved about the subject. However, getting her students to perceive it this way was a different story. They always seemed bored and restless in her class.

As she explained the procedures, some students appeared to be daydreaming while others displayed undisguised irritation. Most disheartening of all were the students who had the courage—or temerity—to express their discontentment about the subject. No one seemed to be having a good time.

Kristen wanted her students to see the importance of math and to be eager to learn it. She also wished they would realize that with a little application, they could comprehend this complex subject and even enjoy it. But somehow, her efforts never seemed to produce the desired effect. What's more, she had begun to take her students' lack of interest as a personal affront. Perhaps, she thought, she just wasn't cut out to be a teacher.

CONNECTING THE DOTS

Boredom, disinterest, blatant disregard—as frustrated as Kristen was by her students' responses (or lack thereof) to her math lessons, their unrelentingly negative attitudes are rather predictable. Equally frustrated and intimidated by a subject they find incomprehensible and of no practical use, her students need a little help in understanding not only the content, but also the value of it.

An aspect of education reform overlooked by many teachers, clarification of the content's value is as important for students as the content itself. Establishing a clear connection between the content and its relevance—and further, between the content and the tools needed for mastery—can remove students' trepidation about dealing with it, making it at once more accessible to them and more interesting. All this is achieved simply because you've connected the dots for them.

Kristen's mistake was in assuming that the students would automatically recognize the significance and relevance of math. Viewing these as obvious attributes, she never considered that her students might perceive it differently. However, she has to make that connection for them in order to ignite their interest and encourage their perseverance. All Kristen needs is a few adjustments to her presentation.

Of course, the starting point is in conveying the content comprehensibly. But students need more than mere comprehension of the subject matter. Recognizing that there actually is a point to what they're doing (and understanding what the point is) makes the content worth pursuing. Thus, they are less likely to gripe about undertaking it and more willing to cooperate—perhaps even to like it.

A good way to begin connecting the dots is to explain to students what content knowledge is essential and why. Then apply the information directly to their lives. Therefore, connecting the dots should include the following:

- The importance of the content
- The skills needed to master the content
- The relevance of the content for students
- The link between the content and other subjects

When Kristen draws the dots and connects them, her students will begin to take a greater interest in acquiring the content knowledge simply because they understand not only the content, but also its significance and its role in their own lives. There go the negative attitudes and querulous comments. Of course, this applies in your classroom as well.

THE IMPORTANCE OF THE CONTENT

Let's begin with the query put forth by Kristen's student: "Why do we have to learn this?" The real question is whether you have a clear and lucid response ready. In fact, if you've never before given genuine thought to the overall importance of your subject's content, now is the time to do so. Moreover, at the start of a semester, you need to be able to illuminate the following for your students:

• The basic premise of the content (which goes directly to the heart of the question)
• Specific reasons for mastering the content
• The short- and long-range benefits of learning the content

Armed with this information at the outset, students are more favorably disposed to gathering content knowledge, even if they're not necessarily attracted to it. Besides, the fact is that students must learn certain skills, information, and concepts, regardless of their desire to do so; they should at least know why.

Taking only a few minutes of your time, your willingness to go the extra mile by clarifying the value of the course conveys respect for your students and their time, intelligence and natural curiosity. As a result, you're more likely to gain exactly what Kristen sought—students who are engaged from the start and who willingly participate in the course.

THE SKILLS NEEDED FOR MASTERY

What sometimes intimidates students about subjects that they find difficult or unappealing—and provokes those peevish laments—is their belief that they lack the skill to be successful in that subject. Their behaviors serve as a defense against anticipated failure. However, teachers can change that mindset.

Therefore, your next step in connecting the dots is to demonstrate to your students that they have the fundamental skills (or that you will assist in their acquisition of these) needed for mastery of the content. Initially, your students may be unaware of two important facts:

• Many complex procedures and ideas form from smaller ones that they already know. By demonstrating to your students that rudimentary tools can be the building blocks for comprehending larger concepts, you make the content more approachable for them. For example, students in a geography or history class need basic map skills and an understanding of the location of countries in order to put cultural issues in context and to understand world events both past and present.

- Students may merely need to gain basic knowledge as the undergirding for more creative pursuits. In an English class, for instance, students need rudimentary knowledge of grammar and sentence structure before they can compose a glorious sonnet or develop a persuasive essay.

Guiding students to find the smaller concepts within the grand ideas or to master the essential tools for creative expression will go a long way toward providing the foundation for mastery of the broader content. Once they realize they possess the mechanics for larger concepts, you have their attention.

Additionally, helping your students to use the skills they have or to acquire the basic skills they may lack for your course content—despite the fact that, perhaps, they should have these skills already at this point in their academic careers—you empower them and even embolden them to be more successful in your course.

Some tips for helping your students gain mastery are:

- Determine the core skills needed to navigate your course content successfully. Then meld these basic skills into your lessons on a frequent and ongoing basis. The repetition will reinforce the skills, thereby preparing your students to use them for more advanced work.
- Develop activities and projects that interweave these basic skills with more advanced skills, in various contexts. This enables students to view the skills from several perspectives as well as to understand how skills are interrelated and interdependent. Using fundamental map skills, for instance—compass rose, longitude and latitude—students can then apply these skills to plot the war campaigns of generals, analyze battle strategy, determine foreign policies of nations, etc., in a history class.
- Use domain-specific terminology regularly with your students so that they become familiar with it and will recognize it, even outside of the context of the course. For instance, your reference to and explanation of muted colors in an art class, becomes a recognizable concept when a character in a novel is referred to as mute or even when the term is used for electronics, as in mute buttons on telephones and in remote controls for televisions. Thus, a term learned in a course offers students connections across academic domains and in non-educational contexts as well.
- Require that your students use their specialized vocabulary in responding to class questions, while participating in class discussions and when developing essays. Doing this provides another layer of reinforcement of foundational skills.

The essential emphasis here is on ways to make complex subject matter accessible to your students. Ultimately, your course should be so reachable that they forget their misgivings and savor the sense of accomplishment that mastery brings. And in the eyes of your students, aren't you the stellar teacher for helping them to discover this!

HIGHLIGHT THE CONTENT'S RELEVANCE

In classrooms everywhere, some of the students lack interest, motivation, and initiative. A multitude of reasons explains these behaviors, many of which are beyond the purview of teachers. However, an area in which teachers can make significant inroads is in the relevance of the materials they teach.

Sometimes failing to perceive any link between the information presented and their individual lives, students deem the material irrelevant. Having so labeled it, students find the content useless and, in their estimation, not worth pursuing. By connecting the dots between the content and students' lives, you have another opportunity to open your students' eyes—and minds—to the joys of learning your subject.

Students need to see a clear correlation, for example, between their own lives and the history teacher's lesson on people who are long dead, the English teacher's lesson on seemingly unfathomable Shakespearean language and the geometry teacher's lesson on postulates and theorems. Without these connections, many students tune out. And behavior problems are sure to ensue.

Recall, for instance, the science experiments that Jason enthusiastically introduced to his students in the beginning of chapter three. A means for making science come alive, science was now relevant to them, which explains why they responded with enthusiasm.

To achieve the same, try some of these suggestions:

- Include creative expression in your lessons. For example, instead of simply reading dialogue from a literature textbook or a world language text, students might work in pairs to develop their own dialogue and perform it in class; history students might role-play a historic debate or reenact a battle; science students might devise their own experiments (all within guidelines that you establish). When students actively participate in formulating their own learning—as underscored throughout this book—the experience is more personal and, therefore, becomes more relevant.
- Highlight the applicability of the content to the students' individual goals and aspirations. You might point out that grammar lessons that students

find tedious, for instance, will sharpen their interviewing skills when applying for a summer job, enabling them to speak articulately and write cogently. Likewise, you might demonstrate the usefulness of mathematical concepts in daily tasks from retail transactions to cooking measurements. The point is to reveal the daily practicality of the content and its role in achieving students' objectives.

- Appeal to your students' intellectual vanity. Students, like adults, appreciate being perceived as intelligent (though not excessively so when interacting with their peers). Therefore, as odd as this suggestion sounds, your demonstration that your course content will enhance their intellectual image immediately makes the material more relevant. Students take pride and pleasure in being the "knowledgeable" one, and this provides an excellent opportunity to do so.

In much the same way as a customer might ask, "What's in it for me?" before signing an agreement, secondary-level students sometimes take this approach to school in general and especially to the classes in which they have little or no interest. Therefore, like a salesperson, a teacher might want to extol the future benefits of this "transaction."

Essentially, by spotlighting the relevance of your course on a personal level, you make the course more attractive to your students. This piques their interest and reduces apathetic (or antagonistic) responses. They then enjoy the process of learning again, unaware that they have been coaxed into it.

LINK CONTENT WITH OTHER SUBJECTS

Let's continue to connect those dots. An interdisciplinary approach to content is another method of making this connection and assisting your students in better relating to the material as well. Often thinking of their courses in isolation, teachers inadvertently lead students to do the same. However, given insight into the interconnectedness of subjects, students gain a means of applying their knowledge in more than one context, which adds to its interest.

As when we noted earlier that students need the ability to transfer knowledge of terminology learned in one course to application in other venues, it's equally important that students understand that concepts have that same transferability from subject to subject. Being able to see these connections can ease students' acquisition of new information in other subjects. Besides, there is the added advantage of helping your students become more well rounded academically as they traverse these porous educational boundaries.

Some techniques for linking content are:

- Expand students' knowledge by overlapping disciplines in unusual, but appropriate, ways. A world language teacher, for instance, might incorporate various modes of artistic expression from the language's country of origin, as well as background on the culture of the people and the sociological and historical factors that contributed to these art forms—all taught in the appropriate language, of course. In so doing, students' knowledge expands in art, cultural geography and sociology or history as they gain proficiency in a second language and broaden their vocabulary in both languages.
- Use students' prior knowledge. Students' knowledge in one area can be a springboard for learning in another. For example, a lesson on a particular period of history can provide the background story for a pertinent literary piece. In a different vein, having strong language skills in a student's native language (e.g. English) makes the acquisition of a second language far easier, particularly when students note the cognates (i.e. words that are identical or quite similar in different languages).
- Align your subject matter with that of another teacher. Science and math teachers, for instance, have enough common areas to make coordination of their subjects' topics doable, just as English and social studies teachers have. This allows the math teacher to provide the mathematical concepts that are the basis for scientific equations. It also encourages the social studies teacher to integrate into the lesson an excerpt from a literary work that coincides with the portion of history that students are studying at that time. Doing this clearly delineates for students exactly how subjects intertwine.
- Apply content to world events. For example, you might apply history course content to a new scientific advancement. Demonstrating not only how history impacts the present, you also show students how they might use the combined information to participate in an intelligent conversation on the topic and even enlighten adults (particularly their parents!) about world events. Having done this, you have connected the content to another subject, simultaneously making the course quite relevant and augmenting students' self-image as well.

By demonstrating the interconnectedness and interdependence of subjects, you broaden your students' view of learning and their perspective on the subjects they learn. You also make learning more interesting, which as you know, is our whole point.

Overall, when you take the time to connect the dots for your students, you make learning more accessible, the content more useful and the entire process more enjoyable. This aspect of reform requires a bit more effort from the teacher, but it makes a significant impact on student motivation and achievement. That's why students will want to be in your class.

Chapter Four: Connect the Dots **Worksheet**

1. What are the most important aspects of the course I teach?

_____

_____

_____

_____

_____

_____

_____

_____

_____

_____

_____

_____

2. What fundamental skills do my students need for success in my course?

_____

_____

_____

_____

_____

_____

_____

_____

_____

_____

_____

_____

_____

_____

Chapter Four: Connect the Dots **Worksheet**

3. How can I help my students to enhance or acquire these skills?.

_____

_____

_____

_____

_____

_____

_____

_____

_____

_____

_____

_____

4. What are the short- and long-range benefits for my students in learning this content?

_____

_____

_____

_____

_____

_____

_____

_____

_____

_____

_____

_____

_____

Chapter Four: Connect the Dots   **Worksheet**

5. How can my students apply this content in their own lives?

_____

_____

_____

_____

_____

_____

_____

_____

_____

_____

_____

6. How can I link my content with real-world issues?

_____

_____

_____

_____

_____

_____

_____

_____

_____

_____

_____

_____

_____

Chapter Four: Connect the Dots **Worksheet**

7. How can I demonstrate the connection between my content and other subjects?

_____

_____

_____

_____

_____

_____

_____

_____

_____

_____

8. Which other teachers will I ask to be a partner with me in aligning our subjects for the benefit of our students? And what topics might we commingle?

_____

_____

_____

_____

_____

_____

_____

_____

_____

_____

_____

_____

Chapter Four: Connect the Dots   **Worksheet**

9. What other suggestions in this chapter will I employ in my classroom?

_____

_____

_____

_____

_____

_____

_____

_____

_____

_____

_____

10. What was the result of my implementation of these suggestions?

_____

_____

_____

_____

_____

_____

_____

_____

_____

_____

_____

Chapter 5

Guess Who's Coming to Class

As the bell rang signaling the start of the school day, Todd rose from his desk and quickly walked to the doorway of his classroom. After all these years of teaching, he still had the same enthusiasm with which he first began. And today, a special sense of anticipation filled him as he awaited the arrival of his government students.

Amid their usual joking and animated conversations, his students took their seats. Gradually, voices faded and all eyes turned toward the front of the room, fixed on the stranger who had arrived unnoticed and now stood beside their teacher. The unknown man chatted quietly with Todd, out of student earshot, as they looked on.

"Who is that?" several students wondered aloud.

"What is he doing here?" others asked.

Answers to their questions came moments later when Todd introduced the stranger as a former FBI agent. The first of several guest speakers, Todd had invited him to address his students as part of their unit on roles in government.

Twitters of excitement spread throughout the room as the agent began addressing the class. Describing a typical day for him, he also shared the more salient portions of his clandestine career. The students hung on every word, enraptured as he spoke, and then riddled him with questions afterward.

Completely engrossed in the discussion, a collective groan arose from the students when the bell rang to end the period. Their response told Todd that, without a doubt, he had hit on something genuinely inspiring with his guest speaker idea. He hoped to equal this level of success as he repeated the venture with other speakers over the next couple of weeks.

OPEN YOUR CLASSROOM DOOR

Judging by the resounding approval of his students, Todd's idea to invite guest speakers was a triumph. The students appreciated the novelty of interacting with a unique guest speaker who brought content information to life through first-person experience. Eliciting their sincere interest and excitement, the recounting of those experiences provided a good deal of new knowledge in a vibrant way unmatched by a textbook.

This easy change spices up routine lessons. Todd's guest-speaker program could be beneficial to virtually any secondary teacher. At least worth considering, by inviting others to share their experiences and skills with your class, you provide your students:

- firsthand knowledge
- new perspectives from "experts"
- useful information that can prove invaluable
- an opportunity to meet living examples of what they've previously only encountered in textbooks
- an introduction to professions to which they may not have been exposed
- the opportunity to ask questions of an expert
- the chance to meet a possible mentor for students contemplating a similar career path
- discovery of their own hidden talents and untapped interests
- fresh voices

Moreover, by interacting with your guest speakers, your students learn on a more personal level—both an inspirational and transformative experience—as they converse with professionals who have enjoyed their chosen professions and attained a certain level of success within them.

Having no genuine downside to this endeavor, in fact, the only potential pitfalls are a disengaged speaker or disinterested students. Teachers can counteract both of these situations by interjecting appropriate questions, comments, and rejoinders as the need arises. So there's little to thwart your plans and a great deal to support them, if you choose to invite outside speakers.

In view of these advantages, consider the following benefits you will accrue, as a teacher, by including guests as part of your lessons:

- A resource with information that you may not possess
- An added dimension to your lessons that breaks from the routine

- A means for making your course content more pertinent and, therefore, more relevant for your students
- A potential partner for future educational undertakings
- An experience that can be an impetus for future class discussions
- A respite from being the daily speaker

The good that comes of inviting outside speakers to your classroom is clear. Therefore, having decided to proceed with the idea, the first step, of course, is to find speakers. Here are a few additional considerations:

- Choose speakers appropriate to your topic and your students' age
- Develop partnerships within the community
- Invite students' family members as speakers
- Include artists from the community

CHOOSE APPROPRIATE SPEAKERS

Deciding to develop a guest-speaker program, you must then determine who the most appropriate speakers are for your students. Eloquence and experience in public speaking need not be important considerations. Instead, the most important factor is that the speakers connect—however loosely—to your subject area and have the ability to do the same with your students. Thus, the more creatively you approach this endeavor the better.

For instance, the obvious choice for guest speaker in a math class would be a mathematician or an accountant. While either would be a fine choice, many other interesting professions incorporate math without it being the primary aspect of the job. Therefore, an architect or a carpenter might prove to be excellent selections by a more innovative math teacher. This teacher also wouldn't want to bypass the interior designer nor the baker, both of whom rely on significant mathematical elements in their work.

Continuing to think beyond the usual parameters, an English teacher should consider those other than the expected authors, poets, and journalists. Remember not to overlook the public relations representative who writes numerous press releases, or the advertising executive who writes the catchy phrases for commercials. Speakers such as these compel students to think of writing in a completely different way.

Regardless of your subject, find speakers who

- Stretch your students' thinking on more than one level (e.g. content, profession, avocation, their own talents and abilities, etc.)
- Provide greater depth on at least one topic covered in your textbook or lectures
- Enlarge your students' perspectives on what your subject covers
- Demonstrate real-world links between the content and the profession
- Show your students how they can use this profession as a career path or simply as an interesting pursuit

At the conclusion of each speaker's presentation, be sure to allot time for students' questions. A successful guest speaker's presentation provides students with a deeper knowledge of the content they are studying, as well as a greater awareness of this profession's connection to it.

Additionally, as you design your program, try to broaden the range of careers presented to encompass those that may not require a professional degree. Your students can gain a treasure trove of knowledge from speakers in skilled professions such as construction, auto mechanics, culinary arts and many other rewarding fields. Think unconventionally, therefore, when pondering careers that link to your academic domain.

Now aware of who constitutes an appropriate speaker for your students, the next factor is where and how to obtain your speakers. Let's view a few options.

DEVELOP PARTNERSHIPS WITHIN THE COMMUNITY

Local businesses and community leaders are excellent resources for teachers seeking classroom speakers. Valuing the chance to share their experiences and wealth of knowledge with others, particularly within their own community, many business owners are happy to accept the invitation to address students.

With this in mind, community leaders frequently welcome the prospect of extending a helping hand to students because

- It's sound business practice for these entrepreneurs to nurture community relationships. Support of local schools is an easy way for business owners to reach out to the community and, in return, to increase business.
- They have at their disposal services, information, and other experts—all of which they are often eager to share, as they gain the goodwill of the community. Obviously, this could prove very beneficial to your students as well.

- Add to this the fact that your students are a potential source of future employees for these businesses. Therefore, the owners have a stake in developing positive relationships with your students now.

You might as well avail yourself of this ready opportunity. All you need do is ask. Business owners and community leaders are usually well prepared for speaking engagements and ready to help in myriad other ways. And as an outgrowth of this initial partnership, you're likely to spark greater school involvement by these entrepreneurs and leaders, in a variety of helpful ways.

INVITE STUDENTS' FAMILY MEMBERS TO SPEAK

A rich and often unnoticed resource, students' family members are another excellent option for guest speaking. They represent numerous different skills, professions, and life experiences that can greatly enhance your lessons, build your students' knowledge base, and proffer a unique type of experiential information. Plus, they are usually very willing participants in anything that benefits their children.

When considering family members, parents immediately spring to mind. A fine choice, nevertheless, remember that family is a rather inclusive word, reaching beyond parents to encompass stepparents, adult siblings, grandparents, aunts and uncles, and even godparents as well. In terms of guest speakers, think about extending invitations to any or all of these family connections, as they suit your lesson plans.

To locate prospective participants:

- Inform your students that you are seeking their family members to participate in your guest-speaker project and ask them to submit nominations along with contact information. Then follow up with the nominees.
- During your school's Open House or PTA meetings, mention your guest speaker project and solicit participants through a sign-up sheet at the door.
- Send an e-mail to all your students' parents apprising them of the project and requesting their participation and that of extended family members.
- If your school has a newsletter or newspaper, place a notice in it, making known the fact that you are seeking family members to participate.

As stakeholders in their children's education, and in the larger community in general, students' family members often appreciate being included in the education process. And you'll find their contributions invaluable. Most important of all, the students gain not merely on an educational level, but on a personal level as they take pride in their family's accomplishments and in being given the opportunity to share these with their classmates.

INCLUDE ARTISTS FROM THE COMMUNITY

In your continuing effort to find guest speakers who are sources of information and inspiration, local artists fit the bill wonderfully. Practitioners of the fine arts—painters, musicians, dancers, singers and other artists—as well as writers and poets not only add cultural flavor to our society, but also greatly enliven and enrich our schools. Yet, these are the very areas frequently cut from students' schedules during budget cuts. Moreover, the artistry of these artisans often goes unnoticed by students simply because they are unaware that these talented artists live in their midst. Enlighten your students by inviting these artists into your classroom.

Not only are such local artists frequently available to schools for speaking engagements, but they are often willing to perform their art at the schools as well. For the student who has never been to an art gallery or seen sculpture or attended a dance recital or a play, the opportunity to witness these events first hand is incomparable. And meeting the actual performance artists will prove an unforgettable experience for your students by making content literally come to life.

Additionally, many artists offer venues such as workshops specifically designed for students. This is a wonderful follow-up activity to the speaking engagement, providing students the means to participate in the art themselves. The creative outlet that art affords frequently emboldens the shy student to take part and the less academically adept student to step into the spotlight, perhaps for the first time. Opening new vistas of possibility for these students, it is an avenue for creative expression for all students.

Nevertheless, if you're thinking that artists only fit into the curricula of fine arts teachers, think again. Here's why:

- In a history or geography class, cultural aspects of other continents come to life via the artistry of these guests.
- As an invited speaker, a musician might explain the mathematical aspect of music in a math class, and then expound on the experience of sound such as pitch, timbre and tone in a science class.
- In a business or economics class, a gallery owner might elaborate on art from an entrepreneur's perspective.

Just a few methods for incorporating artists into your curriculum, why not try expanding your concept of what suits your content and invite your speakers accordingly. By inviting guest experts to speak in your classroom—whether through forging ties with community leaders and entrepreneurs or by way of rolling out the welcome mat to your students' relatives—and linking your curriculum to the arts through various artists, you redefine learning in a practical, yet inventive manner.

Never knowing what (or who) they might find in your classroom, this singular change encourages students to arrive in eager anticipation of the adventure. Additionally, instilling this sense of hopeful expectation in your students motivates them to come to class willing to learn and confident that they will enjoy the experience. That readiness is a major factor in learning. After all, this is why they want to be in your class!

Chapter Five: Guess Who's Coming to Class   **Worksheet**

1 What areas in my curriculum are best suited to guest speakers?

_____

_____

_____

_____

_____

_____

_____

_____

_____

_____

_____

_____

_____

2. What seemingly unconventional professions for my subject might actually prove interesting to include in my class?

_____

_____

_____

_____

_____

_____

_____

_____

_____

_____

_____

_____

_____

Chapter Five: Guess Who's Coming to Class **Worksheet**

3. With which business owners might I develop partnerships?

_____

_____

_____

_____

_____

_____

_____

_____

_____

_____

_____

_____

_____

4. Which community leaders might I call on for support?

_____

_____

_____

_____

_____

_____

_____

_____

_____

_____

_____

_____

_____

Chapter Five: Guess Who's Coming to Class   **Worksheet**

5. What methods will I use to enlist the help of my students' families?

_____

_____

_____

_____

_____

_____

_____

_____

_____

_____

_____

_____

_____

_____

6. How can I connect my subject matter with the arts?

_____

_____

_____

_____

_____

_____

_____

_____

_____

_____

_____

_____

_____

_____

Chapter Five: Guess Who's Coming to Class   **Worksheet**

7. Who are some local artists I might contact?

_____

_____

_____

_____

_____

_____

_____

_____

_____

_____

_____

_____

8. What community venues can I use as an extension of my guest speaker program?

_____

_____

_____

_____

_____

_____

_____

_____

_____

_____

_____

Chapter Five: Guess Who's Coming to Class   **Worksheet**

9. What other suggestions in this chapter will I employ in my classroom?

_____

_____

_____

_____

_____

_____

_____

_____

_____

_____

_____

_____

_____

10. What was the result of my implementation of these suggestions?

_____

_____

_____

_____

_____

_____

_____

_____

_____

_____

_____

_____

_____

Chapter 6

Continue to Learn

Carol could almost teach her chemistry class in her sleep. During twenty-five years of teaching, she had established a comfortable routine and remained true to it. In fact, everything she did in her classroom was precisely as she had done it over all these years. The very idea of deviating from these practices made her uneasy—even a bit queasy.

As a new teacher, Carol had wanted to do everything just right. So she had followed all the precepts laid down in her college courses and strictly adhered to every guideline and method she observed as a student teacher. Garnering praise for those early efforts, along with excellent evaluations, Carol resolved to remain in her supervisors' good graces by never diverging in any aspect of her teaching.

At this point in her career, she could practically recite her lesson plans by heart. (She had laminated these plans long ago, so they would remain neat and intact.) And although the binder in which she kept the plans had become a bit dog-eared with time, Carol was proud to say that she still taught from the very first lesson she ever planned.

Similarly, the chemistry experiments she learned as a college student had continued to serve her quite well ever since her first days of teaching. Of course, this meant that Carol saw no reason to alter these experiments even slightly or to add new ones. And any student who had the audacity to complain in her class was quickly silenced with a withering glare from Carol and a sharp, "This is the way it's done."

Satisfied to continue in this manner until she chose to retire, Carol believed that her class ran like a well-oiled machine. And she might have been able to hold on to that belief had a new principal not arrived, and with him, new perspectives and ideologies.

Aghast at the changes, Carol realized she would have to revamp her lesson plans. To add insult to injury, she would now have to accommodate the various forms of technology that teachers in her district were being trained to use. Of course, she truly would have preferred not to attend this training.

To make matters worse, the old, lackluster experiments just would not do any more, either. Instead, Carol and the other science teachers were sent to a series of workshops on dramatic new experiments—many of them involving the dreaded technology—which teachers also were now expected to incorporate into their lessons. She had had enough.

Having neither the desire nor the inclination to change with the times, Carol felt increasingly uncomfortable and disoriented amidst all the changes. She thought, perhaps, it was time to leave teaching. Yet, after so many years, she couldn't imagine leaving the profession.

WHY SHOULD YOU CHANGE?

Carol's rigid adherence to her routines and her fear of change are not unusual. Becoming complacent once they have established procedures that work for them, many teachers are then intimidated by the prospect (or mandate) of learning new methods and then having to change accordingly. This, in part, accounts for resistance to education reform. But, what Carol and many other teachers fail to realize is the benefits for them and their students in adjusting to many educational changes.

Among the advantages of adapting to education reforms are that they:

- Energize teachers who may be slipping toward that precipice of mechanical, rote teaching. Routinized instruction, while easy, also encourages teachers to forego novel approaches and new trends in favor of maintaining the status quo. Being required to change can reinvigorate teachers and, by extension, the lessons they teach.
- Encourage teachers to progress with the times and remain abreast of new educational techniques. Without change, it's easy to become anachronistic. While the familiar may become comfortable, teachers shouldn't allow their methods and practices to become outdated.
- Add to any teacher's repertoire. It's always good pedagogy to acquire new skills and ideas and then combine them with the tried and true. This enlarges the teacher's supply of lessons and activities while at once refreshing them as well.
- Augment students' learning and increases their interest in the subject matter by adding contemporary elements to the lessons. Often more familiar

with computers and other technological devices than adults are, students are comfortable using them and welcome their incorporation in lessons.

Therefore, threatening though change may initially be to some teachers' comfort levels, it's necessary for continued growth as an educator. In overcoming any natural reticence you may have about stepping beyond your traditional methods and removing your self-imposed boundaries, you may be surprised to discover that learning new methodologies and implementing them in your classroom is not nearly as intimidating as you might have anticipated. Furthermore, the fresh techniques and perspectives that you gain can definitely enhance your students' educational experience.

However, even if you're willing to consider new ideas and methods, you still need to know where to find them. Among the numerous places to look are:

• Workshops that specifically target your subject, as well as those for professional development
• Education conferences
• Membership in professional organizations
• Your colleagues
• Web sites, books and supplementary materials

Opportunities abound to learn new ideas, techniques, and practices. After delving into them, you can determine which ones work best for you. Retain what works and discard the rest. Having greatly benefited from the experience, you'll be less likely to feel intimidated by the next wave in education. And, rest assured, there will be another educational wave very soon!

ATTEND AN EDUCATION WORKSHOP

A good place to begin and a perfect example of practice what you preach are workshops. Spending a good deal of time exhorting their students to continue learning, educators can avail themselves of that same opportunity to remain lifelong learners by attending education workshops. Additionally, whether it's the latest technological advancement or a new way to teach an old lesson, attending a workshop can become a stimulus for developing your own new practices and, at the very least, a means of rejuvenating your professional outlook.

The fact is that any subject or grade that you've taught long enough can become mundane. And although it's reassuring to have your lessons and activities already prepared and readily available, as Carol did in the anecdote at the outset of this chapter, without reworking those lessons and activities from time to time, and learning ways to make them fresh and interesting, even you will become bored with your own lessons. And that boredom can affect your teaching as well as your morale. This is where workshops can be helpful.

Here's why:

- Workshops offer a variety of topics and hands-on learning opportunities in a condensed time span.
- The short duration of workshops minimizes your time away from class and maximizes your learning potential.
- Workshops often provide supplementary materials such as books and DVD's that you can integrate into your planning to add another layer of interest to your lessons.

Of course, a workshop of your own choosing has the greatest probability of being both constructive and appealing to you. Additionally, it's worth noting that each of the assorted types of workshops provides unique benefits. The focus of subject-specific workshops on enriching the content, for example, is apt to draw your interest if your methodology is already current and you now want to electrify the content.

On the other hand, professional development workshops with a pedagogical emphasis often offer cutting-edge methodologies, progressive ideas, and fresh viewpoints that can enrich your teaching practices. Both of these types of workshops can prove valuable.

Moreover, although all teachers must occasionally attend mandated workshops that would not otherwise be their preference, these can be equally beneficial. Gleaning the gems of information, useful tools and pertinent materials amidst the dross can become a professional treasure hunt under such circumstances. Yet, once found, these make your attendance at mandated workshops worthwhile. Therefore, whether it's a mandated workshop or one that you have chosen to attend, view them as professional opportunities.

RECONSIDER EDUCATION CONFERENCES

The ubiquity of education conferences may compel you to conclude that you've already attended enough of them. Add to this the monotony of some conference speakers—provoking attendees to lament the expenditure of time and money—and you might well decide to bypass them. This would be a mistake.

Despite their reputation to the contrary, it is quite plausible that you will leave an education conference even more committed to the education profession than when you arrived and proud to be associated with such a learned group of people. It all depends on which conferences you choose to attend. And the operative word here is "choose."

Therefore, don't hesitate to include education conferences among your resources for improvement. Assuming that your preference is to leave the conference fulfilled, it pays to be selective. Here are some considerations when attending education conferences:

- Just as with workshops, look for those that pertain to your subject first. These present a superb opportunity to hear subject-specific speakers and receive superior resource materials that school districts sometimes cannot afford to offer.
- Of course, education conferences that are pedagogical in nature are also a great choice. Like professional development workshops, conferences that focus on pivotal education issues and methods to improve education can enable you to return to class with state-of-the-art theories and the means to implement them.
- Learn about the advantages of various professional organizations associated with the conference and/or its sponsors. Then obtain information on the benefits of membership in these organizations. We'll discuss this in more depth shortly.
- From the smaller "break-out" sessions within these conferences, select those offering topics that not only interest you but also challenge you to expand your skills and/or knowledge base.
- Use this opportunity to connect with your peers in neighboring communities, as you would in workshops, as well as those in other parts of the country. This may provide opportunities for mutual professional support, as well as for cooperative endeavors between your students and theirs as another byproduct of the education conference.

Returning with new ideas and a bright outlook, your upbeat attitude may be transferrable to your students. And anything that promotes a more enlivened and stimulating classroom atmosphere is worth pursuing. Often, education conferences do exactly that.

JOIN A PROFESSIONAL ORGANIZATION

As mentioned earlier, professional organizations can be advantageous to you as an educator. Whether directly or indirectly, these organizations assist you in the classroom. Therefore, even if you're generally reluctant to join groups or organizations, this reason alone makes them worthy of your consideration. And here are a few other reasons:

- Professional organizations give you a chance to meet and mingle with superlative colleagues—classroom innovators and leaders—whom you might not otherwise encounter. Simply having the opportunity to speak with, and be influenced by, those who are doing new and fascinating things makes this membership worthwhile.
- The exchange of information, sharing of techniques, and discussion of leading-edge educational trends and issues is priceless. These can support your classroom goals and elevate your lessons to a much more dynamic level.
- The members offer another potential source of guest speakers/experts to address your classes, as discussed in chapter five. In turn, you may serve in the same capacity for other teachers and gain from the experience of being in a different classroom setting.

While your schedule—not just in school but in life—may preclude devoting large amounts of time to the meetings and other activities that often accompany membership in organizations, you may opt to participate to the extent that you are comfortable. This still allows you to partake of whatever is most personally enriching.

Ultimately, experiencing novel education opportunities, you become more well rounded and, therefore, a better teacher. Furthermore, in much the same way as your students' education is expanded by visiting relevant venues, as suggested in chapter two, and by meeting and learning from guest speakers/ mentors, as put forth in chapter five, your professional growth can receive a considerable boost by your interaction with other educators in workshops, conferences and organizations. And your improvements offer a subsequent benefit to your students as well.

SEEK OUT COLLEAGUES

While we're on the subject of learning from others, keep in mind your colleagues in your own school. Easily overlooked just by dint of their familiarity, among your colleagues are fonts of information, if you only ask. So, ask.

As you become more acquainted with your co-workers, identifying the standouts among them is easy. These teachers retain their enthusiasm for their subject over the years, along with their love of learning and a genuine concern for their students. Not succumbing to every new educational fad or technological novelty, these teachers nonetheless incorporate fresh ideas and techniques into their lessons and take pleasure in being able to introduce these to their students. In short, these outstanding teachers genuinely enjoy teaching.

These stellar teachers are the ones you want to seek out. Not surprisingly, they are usually the ones most willing to impart their knowledge, experience and expertise. Therefore, embolden yourself to ask for:

- Methods for maintaining your enthusiasm over the long haul
- Techniques for keeping students involved and interested
- Ideas on how you might freshen activities that you already use in your lessons
- The workshops, conferences and organizations they have found most professionally helpful (and why)
- Whether they would be willing to observe and critique your teaching methods
- And, perhaps most important, whether they will permit you to observe their teaching in action once or twice

Just a few among the many ways in which you can learn from fellow educators, these requests form a good starting point. Moreover, your colleagues are likely to be flattered by your respect for their professional efforts. Therefore, consider what you might learn from the best teachers in your school and become a willing pupil.

SURF THE INTERNET

In this technological age, direct contact with other educators is clearly not a teacher's only source of information. The proliferation of the Internet has made it the resource of choice for many people seeking to learn new things in much the same way as encyclopedias once played this role in days gone by. This makes the Internet an obvious choice for teachers seeking to gain new insights, discover the latest theories, find creative lesson plans or just spice up their old lessons with innovative projects and activities.

Among the simple yet useful means of employing the Internet are the following:

- From lesson planning to augmenting projects to researching topics, Internet search engines have become the preferred means of gathering information. Galileo, for instance, a superb academic search engine, provides academic research for teachers and students alike. Although it requires a password, many school systems subscribe to this excellent resource, which is where the password can be obtained.

- In planning lessons, search engine websites such as Google, bing and yahoo are also great resources. Simply enter a key phrase such as "lesson plans," plus your subject area. The resulting plethora of plans and ideas from which you may then choose will enable you to select the ones best suited to your objectives and plans.
- Likewise, by entering the name of your subject area in the search box of the aforementioned websites, along with the words "projects" or "activities," a vast array of assignments, ready for use in your classroom, is summoned by your fingertips. From this large selection, several from which you might draw inspiration, as well as those that would meld seamlessly into your lessons are sure to spring up.
- Designed explicitly to cater to teachers, various websites offer answers to pedagogical questions, sample lesson plans, and even suggestions on classroom management.

As a source of information and insight, the Internet makes teachers' job easier by literally placing so much professional assistance at your fingertips. Its ability to broaden your own education and stimulate that of your students is virtually limitless.

DON'T OVERLOOK TRADITIONAL OUTLETS

As invaluable as the Internet is as a resource, the traditional learning routes are still excellent choices for teachers brainstorming ways to reform education creatively, on an individual level. Long preceding the proliferation of technology in our classrooms, college courses and supplementary books were the natural means by which teachers learned new trends and techniques.

Their low-tech characteristics placing them squarely in the "old-school" category, there is, nevertheless, no valid reason for today's teachers to forego resource books as educational sources. Indeed, they have a good deal to offer a contemporary teacher in that:

- Many provide complete lessons that often include great activities
- They frequently provide helpful hints and tips to enliven lessons that you may have previously developed
- They are a very cost-effective means of educating yourself, making them an even bigger draw.

College courses, of course, are the place where teachers receive their basic training. Also a great source for ongoing education, they enable educators to keep up with the changing times. In fact, if Carol (in the scenario that opened this chapter) had continued to take an occasional course, she might not have been so overwhelmed and frightened by the educational alterations she experienced when her school's administration changed.

Attending a college course from time to time will:

- Expose you to educational trends.
- Inform you of new educational terminology, which would otherwise be intimidating if you are unfamiliar with it.
- Enable you to interact with teachers of different ages and educational settings (e.g. public school vs. private school). This may prove enlightening, thereby informing your own teaching.
- Strengthen the skills you already possess, while developing new ones.

FINDING TIME

With the responsibility to be both a knowledgeable instructor and a perpetual student, learning is a never-ending process for educators. However, before you cast this book aside, certain that it places inordinate demands on your time, wait. Not intended to further burden overworked teachers, this chapter's suggestions are that workshops, conferences, and the like become a way of making your job easier and more enjoyable rather than consuming all your free time.

Countless options exist regarding when, where, and from whom you learn; simply exercise your options. Select and attend what you deem to be most intriguing and advantageous to you and your students. Disregard the rest.

Acquiring the knowledge to improve your skills, you can then hone your craft and make your class more fascinating for everyone concerned. Furthermore, with only a modest expenditure of time, teachers who continue to learn are able to use that learning to effect education reform in their own classrooms—reform that is appealing and productive.

Chapter Six: Continue to Learn   **Worksheet**

1. As an experienced teacher, what areas can I change to make my teaching more current?

_____

_____

_____

_____

_____

_____

_____

_____

_____

_____

_____

_____

2. As a novice teacher, what specific steps will I take to prevent stagnating as a teacher?

_____

_____

_____

_____

_____

_____

_____

_____

_____

_____

_____

_____

Chapter Six: Continue to Learn **Worksheet**

3. What are two education workshops that interest me and might prove most useful to me?

_____

_____

_____

_____

_____

_____

_____

_____

_____

_____

_____

_____

4. Which subject-specific conference would I consider attending?

_____

_____

_____

_____

_____

_____

_____

_____

_____

_____

_____

_____

_____

_____

Chapter Six: Continue to Learn   **Worksheet**

5. Which professional development conference, focused on pedagogy, might be beneficial to me?

_____

_____

_____

_____

_____

_____

_____

_____

_____

_____

_____

_____

6. Which professional organizations will I research and consider joining?

_____

_____

_____

_____

_____

_____

_____

_____

_____

_____

_____

_____

_____

_____

Chapter Six: Continue to Learn **Worksheet**

7. Which colleagues might be willing to observe my teaching and allow me to observe theirs?

_____

_____

_____

_____

_____

_____

_____

_____

_____

_____

_____

8. What college courses interest me and are potentially helpful to me professionally?

_____

_____

_____

_____

_____

_____

_____

_____

_____

_____

_____

_____

Chapter Six: Continue to Learn   **Worksheet**

9. What other suggestions in this chapter will I employ in my classroom?

_____

_____

_____

_____

_____

_____

_____

_____

_____

_____

_____

_____

_____

10. What was the result of my implementation of these suggestions?

_____

_____

_____

_____

_____

_____

_____

_____

_____

_____

_____

_____

_____

Chapter 7

Know Your Teaching Style

Dave knew he had a problem, but he wasn't quite sure how to solve it. Somehow, he had lost control of his World Lit class, and creating order and structure seemed just beyond his reach. Coupling his natural exuberance with an unconventional teaching style, he had created an atmosphere in which pandemonium was the norm. The good part was that his students loved being there.

Never really knowing what might occur as they arrived each day, they nonetheless knew there would be a good deal of laughter. Perhaps their teacher would be wearing a multicolored clown wig today and spouting interesting sayings, or maybe he would join them in a game of hacky sack when both he and the students became restless. Maybe he would choose a student to be the brunt of his seemingly endless repertoire of practical jokes, or perhaps he would engage the class in a sing along. Who knew?

Still young—and even more so at heart—Dave's overall goal during his two-year teaching career had always been to have a good time, which is why his students were so enamored of his class. He'd been inspired by a workshop at which teachers were encouraged to be spontaneous and creative. Thus, he made sure to find ways to keep his students entertained. In addition to the jokes, songs, costumes, and games, he enjoyed regaling them with impromptu zany stories and often indulged them in a variety of playful antics. The problem was that laughter and frivolity consumed the entirety of the class period.

What's more, whether any of these jokes, stories and other activities actually corresponded to the current literary piece they were supposed to be studying was generally immaterial to Dave. As long as he was the "good-time" teacher, he savored the position. Of course, this meant that a good deal of learning was lost amid the gaiety, creating an even greater problem.

Despite the aura of "coolness" bestowed upon him by his students, Dave had begun to realize that he lacked credibility among his colleagues. What he meant as good-natured amusement was seen by them as an inability to manage a classroom. In fact, perceived by his students more as a peer than an authority figure, maintaining order had become somewhat of an issue in his class. Moreover, Dave's reputation for pranks and games gave other teachers the distinct impression that he was less than competent as an educator.

Desiring the respect of his colleagues and a more educational atmosphere in his classroom, Dave wanted to infuse his classes with a bit of the order he had seen other teachers employ in their classrooms which, he believed, would enable him to spend more time on actual teaching. On the other hand, he was unwilling to relinquish his classroom's liveliness for what he perceived as solemnity and boredom, and he didn't want to lose the spontaneity and joviality for which he was known. Unable to figure out how to meld these goals, Dave was at an impasse.

BALANCE IS FUNDAMENTAL

While everything in this book advocates making education a thought-provoking and exhilarating experience for students, the potential hazard of encouraging innovation and creativity is that some teachers will take this recommendation to an extreme, precluding actual education. Dave is just such an example. Heavy on entertainment, his lessons are light on substance. Yet in the midst of his teaching style of mirth and games are some elements worth keeping; they're just buried in the frenetic activity. And therein is the problem.

In an attempt to win his students' approval and to establish a rapport with them, Dave has forgone teaching, for the most part, and elevated amusement in its place. Although his students are thrilled by the constant entertainment, as time has progressed, they have very little knowledge beyond what they had when they first entered his classroom. Thus, Dave's class has essentially become one long recess period and his students' education, along with his professional reputation, has suffered in the process.

While the approval of colleagues should not be a professional goal, being held in low professional regard certainly isn't either. Ultimately, even Dave is not comfortable with the teaching style he has created. He hasn't yet learned how to make learning the focus and entertainment the bonus. This principal balance is the cornerstone of the reform offered here.

Although Dave's attempts to implement the new techniques and methodologies he acquired at a professional development workshop are commendable—actually, acquiring new skills is the primary purpose of continuing the professional learning we discussed in chapter six—he has misunderstood the role of these innovations. Their function is enhancement of education, not replacement of it. Instead, Dave has become a great success as an entertainer, but not as a teacher. Fortunately, to his credit, he realizes this.

As a young educator, you might find yourself in similar circumstances—working diligently to make your course interesting, yet overlooking classroom management and serious learning in the process. Conversely, if you are a veteran educator, you may discover that you've tried too hard to prohibit any levity from entering your lessons in order to maintain control and remain on-task. Yet, neither extreme supports the academic exploration and genuine acquisition of knowledge that make active learning a vibrant experience. So, a little balance is in order.

Clearly, balance is the missing ingredient in Dave's teaching style. Between the revelry currently occurring in his class and the extreme quiet and rigidity he fears rests the perfect equilibrium. A few simple adjustments will bring about this symbiosis of order and amusement. Then Dave will have an engaging and distinctive teaching style that produces measurable learning. So can you.

To achieve this balance, here are a few essential considerations:

* Select methods that stretch your comfort zone
* Structure the amusement in your classroom
* Integrate new methods with old ones
* Conform new methods to your teaching style
* Refine your teaching style

Small actions with significant impact, these steps combined make learning exciting, yet within a framework. And you retain your personal teaching style. This education reform benefits everyone involved.

STRETCH YOUR COMFORT ZONE

Dave was more than happy to integrate all sorts of merriment into his lessons because these types of lessons suited not only his personality but also his teaching style. As such, they were squarely in his comfort zone. Not problematic in itself, this nonetheless became troublesome, as Dave remained too snugly ensconced in these familiar procedures. He failed to see the advantages that lie in varying his practices, particularly since his usual lacked structure.

In fact, his methods are a cautionary tale of what can occur when teachers fail to develop student-centered rather than teacher-centered lessons. Always standing center stage and in perpetual motion, Dave never realized that he might enjoy his work even more and accomplish more academically if he calmed down and exited the stage occasionally.

Incorporating a few new techniques that differ diametrically from his usual, Dave might allot a portion of the period to lecture, some class discussions, and note taking, to name a few, lending his lessons the structure they so desperately need. Interspersed with the more kinesthetic activities that Dave favors, these tightly constructed portions would be outside his norm but together with the activities, would be far more conducive to genuine learning, yet still enjoyable.

These additions balance the lesson by changing the pace, while also circumventing the overemphasis on frivolity that was superseding learning. In fact, you are likely to find that stretching your own routine procedures to accommodate opposing methods and techniques can improve your teaching as well. Here's why:

- Completely different techniques prevent predictable, stagnant lessons. Whether your usual teaching style is energetic and improvisational, low-key and almost algorithmic, or somewhere in between, trying methods and assignments that are opposite of those you might usually choose revitalizes your current lesson plans and can engender ideas for new lessons.
- Trying methods and techniques outside your norm sharpens your skills. When teachers choose to vary their methodologies, it's very much like an athlete building new muscles by using a new workout routine. Trying new practices compels teachers to build a new set of skills while often simultaneously sharpening existing skills.
- New practices encourage the teacher to remain fully engaged in the lesson. While not a problem for Dave, rote teaching is frequently a side effect of repeatedly using the same lessons or the same techniques. Adding a few new methods engages a teacher's attention simply by virtue of their novelty, often renewing the teacher's enthusiasm at the same time. That enthusiasm will spread to your students.

Stretching your comfort zone to encompass practices and methodologies that contrast sharply with your habitual choices produces lessons that are more balanced—and intriguingly unpredictable.

STRUCTURE THE AMUSEMENT IN YOUR CLASSROOM

As Dave's colleagues have surmised, classroom management has become a major problem for him. While maintaining order and control in a classroom is not the only consideration in lesson planning, as noted in chapter two, it is certainly an important one without which you're unlikely to be able to teach. Of course, as Dave has now discovered, this has an equally adverse effect on learning.

Without squelching his students' enthusiasm, Dave needs to establish structure and guidelines for the engaging activities that he and his students favor. This will allow meaningful education to flourish in a creative environment. Thus, students learn and still enjoy the process.

Some tips for establishing this type of structure include the following changes to your lesson plans:

- Add entertaining undertakings in smaller increments. Rather than devote the majority of every class period to fun and games as Dave has, apportion small segments of class time to a couple of well-chosen activities of only a few minutes' duration. Particularly helpful for teachers who tend to avoid the inclusion of activities in lesson planning, the creative time is within the framework of very organized portions of the lesson, enlivening and balancing it. The intrinsic time constraints of class periods provide an additional degree of organization, once again allaying classroom management issues.
- Alternatively, occasionally use the entirety of one or two class periods, only for assignments that warrant in-depth group research or analysis. Rather than use this type of assignment on a regular basis, a judicious use of period-long assignments, with specific steps included, affords students the necessary time for collaboration. An excellent merger of research, critical thinking skills, and creativity, the use of this suggestion along with the one above, substantially increases students' actual learning time while still adding spice to the lessons.
- Intersperse independent activities with more interactive periods in each lesson. Providing a smooth transition between phases of the lesson, alternating whole-class or small-group activities with independent portions of a lesson redirects students' attention before an exuberant atmosphere becomes an unproductive one. Examples of creative independent activities include students writing different scenarios or new endings for a literary piece in a lit class, working individually to analyze a science experiment or devising a list of review questions for subsequent use in quizzing a partner. Independent but engaging, these types of activities propel the lesson forward without interruption.
- Closely align all activities with the content of your lesson. Dave's mistake of including stories, songs, and jokes was not in these activities themselves, but rather in their lack of coordination with the literature content. Creating or locating only activities and lesson enhancements that match with the specific topic at hand easily alleviates this problem. Now the entertaining aspects of the lesson are also pertinent.

- Plan your lessons well. All of these tips boil down to a well-constructed lesson. Carefully planning each lesson—taking the time to consider the best undertakings that are germane to the content, boost learning and motivate your students—will enable you to achieve the proper balance. Moreover, removing the emphasis on solely interactive activities also brings balance to your lessons, adding a few dashes of enjoyable learning without getting off track. The added benefit is that classroom management issues recede as well.

INTEGRATE NEW METHODS WITH OLD ONES

The prospect of overhauling lesson plans that have proven useful can seem unappealing. The old adage, "If it ain't broke, don't fix it," likely springs to mind. However, since the curriculum you teach is essentially the same year after year, regardless of the subject you teach, there is no need to banish the lessons you have used all these years. Rather, a better choice is to integrate them with new methods, techniques, and activities.

Discovering fresh enhancements that add zest to a lesson plan and perk up student interest is exciting for teachers who want to be innovative, and can inject a shot of enthusiasm into teachers who wouldn't normally consider renovating their lessons. From activities to projects to DVD's to music, these extras can make all the difference between repeating the same old lessons, in the same manner, year after year and presenting lessons that engage the teacher's interest as much as the students.' Therefore, it's worth your expenditure of a little time and effort to review and rejuvenate your lesson plans each year.

Here are some suggestions to help you begin the process:

- In planning a lesson, reassess those you already have on the topic. If these lessons originally lacked any type of enhancement, now is the time to update them. The mere addition of a paired discussion, analysis of a few minutes of music pertaining to the topic or viewing a segment of a relevant DVD can enrich a lesson tremendously for your students.
- A previous lesson, originally including only one activity or other form of augmentation, might benefit from the addition of a second activity of a different variety. In a math class, for example, in addition to demonstrating the teacher's math problems on the board, as may have previously been planned, students might work independently to design their own math problems for classmates to solve. Affording students creative opportunities,

this approach also provides them the chance to review mathematical processes, critique procedures and learn from classmates.

- Replace an unsuccessful activity previously used in an otherwise good lesson with a novel assignment or other endeavor. Salvaging the lesson, this refreshes it for the teacher and makes it more likely to be successful for the students.

- Think beyond the typical. Perhaps this is the time to merge your content with another, as suggested in chapter four, or to teach it experientially in a different venue, as suggested in chapter two. English and music, for instance, may meld beautifully when students who have already learned to develop poetry or creative writing are directed to write poems or prose to be set as lyrics to instrumental pieces playing in the background. Likewise, the reenactment of a great battle may take on new proportions if done outdoors on the lawn.

Thinking of ways to present the usual in an unusual manner lends itself to creative means to make learning more meaningful for your students. And that's the whole point.

CONFORM NEW METHODS TO YOUR TEACHING STYLE

With the strong advocacy presented here for trying and including new techniques and innovations in your lesson plans, the purpose is not for you to abandon your own teaching style. A combination of personality, training, and educational philosophy—plus ideas collated from various sources—teaching style develops over time. This means it can change over time as well. That's why becoming a better teacher—not a completely new one—is the goal.

Weaving your recently acquired practices into your current teaching style, you ensure the most effective use of your new techniques without discarding the core of who you are as a teacher. That's balance, too.

As you step outside your usual teaching routines to diversify your lessons, think of how you can retain your essential concept of teaching while still infusing your content with originality and verve that will motivate your students. Here are some considerations:

- Make changes gradually. Rather than attempt to incorporate every type of activity and technique you find, begin by adding one new practice to each lesson. Start with an easy method or activity and then add others over time. For example, progress from a creative whole class enhancement to innovative small-group projects to more independent paired activities. This gradual progression makes a smooth transition from your basic style of teaching to an upgraded version of it.

- Use whole-class discussions to ease your crossover from a teacher-centered teaching style that relies primarily on lectures to the student-centered practices that enliven teaching. As facilitator of the discussions, you still have a certain level of control, while affording students opportunities for active participation. In addition to discussions, intersperse other types of lesson enhancements with lectures, progressively, thereby stretching your style to accommodate new practices while retaining its essence.
- Use the main concepts that you want to convey in each lesson as a guide to devise or research easy lesson enhancements to underscore these concepts. Then work these enhancements into your lessons in ways that fit naturally with the content and with your teaching style.

Bearing these suggestions in mind, you'll be equipped to strike the proper balance between your teaching style and the innovations you're adding to your lessons. The addition of new methods and activities should allow your teaching style to shine through, making learning more intriguing, challenging and enjoyable for your students. And fully engaged students ultimately make teaching more exhilarating as well.

REFINE YOUR TEACHING STYLE

Ideally, your new practices will help you to refine your teaching style. As you merge your newfound methodologies and activities with your lessons, you're likely to find that you are editing and polishing your style along the way, resulting in a refined version of your original teaching style.

If you are new to teaching, the formation of your teaching style is not yet complete. Having worked as a student teacher, following the example set by the lead teacher, or maybe having only a year or two of teaching experience, enough time has not yet elapsed for you to compile all the factors that influence teaching style. However, your lack of experience can be an asset.

Working very much in your favor is the fact that your manner of teaching is still malleable, enabling you to form it in conjunction with the techniques and practices you choose to employ. Maintaining a balance between your approach to teaching and these lesson enhancements will be easy as the two blend, forming your unique teaching style.

On the other hand, those who have been teaching for a while benefit from their in-depth knowledge of their own basic style. This knowledge provides a strong foundation for selecting the best-suited activities and other lesson enhancements, making the most striking difference in their lessons as they continue to refine their style.

Juxtaposing activities that match your style—whether quiet or interactive—with those that are outside your usual classroom persona, your teaching style is subtly but effectively refined. In so doing, it's also important to keep your lessons well paced and well balanced. Therefore, whether a novice or a veteran, here are some tips for refining your teaching style:

- Change with the times. With the advent of new educational trends, school districts adopt new procedures to which teachers must adhere, as Carol noted in chapter five. Often lasting only until the next new trend arises, these procedures nonetheless may have some attributes that you consider worth keeping. Add them to your educational portfolio, and you refine your teaching style.
- Accommodate your students. As veteran teachers know, each class has a collective personality of its own, which doesn't always mesh well with a teacher's approach to teaching. When this occurs, students must adapt, not the teacher. However, it's wise to assess how your teaching style might best meet the needs of these particular students. Perhaps, for example, this class needs more small-group work, providing necessary interaction in a constructive manner. Or maybe they need more opportunities for quiet, independent study. Refining your teaching style in these instances entails not changing your methodology, but rather carefully selecting which of your methods to use.
- Observe other teachers once again. Taking the time to sit in on the classes of exemplary colleagues whom you admire, as mentioned in chapter six—but this time with an eye toward the style and practices you might emulate—affords you the opportunity to cull their best practices and adapt them in your own way. That's style!
- Review the similarities among your resources. From the Internet to resource books to workshops and conferences, you are likely to note a similar thread running through the practices and activities that appeal to you. They suit your style. Therefore, in building your teaching repertoire, these techniques will become the foundation for your teaching style. Just remember that in order to present interesting and balanced lessons, you need to include additional methods that stretch the confines of your preferences as well.

As you define and refine your teaching style, your teaching will improve, education will become more dynamic in your classroom, and classroom management will be a non-issue. It's all a matter of balance. Just remember to enjoy the process.

Chapter Seven: Know Your Teaching Style   **Worksheet**

1. What is my overall teaching style?

   _____

   _____

   _____

   _____

   _____

   _____

   _____

   _____

   _____

   _____

   _____

   _____

   _____

   _____

2. What methods and activities am I uncomfortable using?

   _____

   _____

   _____

   _____

   _____

   _____

   _____

   _____

   _____

   _____

   _____

   _____

Chapter Seven: Know Your Teaching Style   **Worksheet**

3. How can I update my teaching style to be in step with new educational trends?

_____

_____

_____

_____

_____

_____

_____

_____

_____

_____

_____

4. How might I insert some of these practices in a way that I would be comfortable employing?

_____

_____

_____

_____

_____

_____

_____

_____

_____

_____

Chapter Seven: Know Your Teaching Style   **Worksheet**

5. In what ways can I add balance to my current lesson plans?

_____

_____

_____

_____

_____

_____

_____

_____

_____

_____

_____

_____

_____

6. Which aspects of my current teaching style do I want to be sure to retain?

_____

_____

_____

_____

_____

_____

_____

_____

_____

_____

_____

_____

Chapter Seven: Know Your Teaching Style **Worksheet**

7. What ways will I combine my current methods with new techniques and activities?

_____

_____

_____

_____

_____

_____

_____

_____

_____

_____

_____

8. How will I structure activities in my classroom to prevent management problems?

_____

_____

_____

_____

_____

_____

_____

_____

_____

_____

_____

Chapter Seven: Know Your Teaching Style   **Worksheet**

9. What other suggestions in this chapter will I employ in my classroom?

_____

_____

_____

_____

_____

_____

_____

_____

_____

_____

_____

_____

_____

10. What was the result of my implementation of these suggestions?

_____

_____

_____

_____

_____

_____

_____

_____

_____

_____

_____

_____

_____

Chapter 8

Support Your Students

School had only been in session a month, and Kate already knew it was going to be a tough year. A middle school teacher with several years' experience, she was quite adept at handling the problems typical of this age group. Now, she quickly detected students in nearly all of her French classes who were in need of more than a little help. In addition to the usual struggles with content, behavior issues had risen to the fore.

Freddie, for example, a student in Kate's first period class, was taking French as a third language, after having labored through English as a second language. Verbal dexterity not being his strong suit, Freddie's French pronunciation and attempts at conjugating verbs were proving to be more frustrating than he could handle. Instead of persevering, he had taken to playing the role of class clown, making jokes out of his French mistakes and loudly mocking the more proficient students. Taking his lead, two other boys had begun the same behaviors, the three of them now proving to be distracting and disruptive presences in the classroom.

The third period bell each day ushered in Melissa and Jessica. Archrivals in every arena, they brought their discord to Kate's French class, maintaining an undercurrent of tension and hostility when not verbally sparring. Each highly skilled in her own right, Melissa had the edge in French fluency, while Jessica dominated in mastery of grammar, making her written skills par excellence. The difficult home lives that both girls endured only exacerbated—or perhaps, provoked—their surly temperaments, which was particularly evident when each resorted to sarcastic remarks whenever the other was called upon to speak. Quelling their verbal exchanges was no easy task for Kate as she tried to assist other students who simply lacked the basic skills to be in the class.

Then there was fourth period. A motley assortment of ability levels, Kate had her work cut out for her in attempting to present the curriculum in a manner that was comprehensible to all of them. Adding to Kate's dilemma were the societal issues and family pressures that accompanied many of these students to class; learning French simply did not top their lists of priorities. Sympathetic, even empathetic to their myriad needs, Kate was also determined not to allow any of these issues to take precedence over learning.

Sure, she had read a good deal about creative practices and even had a rather extensive array of activities prepared for her students. Additionally, having attended enough education workshops and conferences on holistic approaches to teaching, Kate knew that simply ignoring the student's non-academic issues was not an option. So she also had researched techniques for working with students like hers, whose personal problems precluded academic effort. But none of those education experts taught in her school, under the conditions she faced every day. No one really knew the enormity of the task before her.

Feeling dismayed but not defeated, Kate began to lay out her plan of action, devising ways to reach and teach each student.

STUDENTS ARE INDIVIDUALS FIRST

The assortment of classroom difficulties facing Kate is not uncommon. They are also not as onerous as some that other teachers face. Yet, they are obstacles to learning. And without a magic wand to dispel the difficulties, it's tempting to throw your hands up in despair when students' problems seem too numerous or too burdensome. However, Kate has the right idea: make a plan.

She's also right in noting that although she's attended education conferences and read countless books, the experts who expound on pedagogy aren't in her classroom, confronting the complex mixture of societal issues, content struggles and typical adolescent personality conflicts set before her. In fact, transporting advice from books and workshops to the real world of teaching is not always an easy journey. Nonetheless, this needn't deter you.

At the outset, it's important to note that not every problem presented by a student is within the purview of teachers. Contrary to popular opinion, teachers cannot heal all of society's ills. However, to the extent that these outside factors hinder or inhibit students' learning, it is the teacher's concern and responsibility to take action—one student at a time.

Attempting to address the problems en masse is a blueprint for failure. First, doing this presupposes that problems supersede the individuals that bear them and further, that a teacher can resolve all problems in one fell swoop. It doesn't happen that way. And in instances such as Kate's—contending with several problems, different ones in each class—trying to come up with one solution for all the problems is a futile endeavor that dehumanizes students and increases a teacher's stress.

So, what is the solution? Look beyond the surface issues to see the person battling in the midst of them. A combination of sensitivity to students' difficulties and building support systems within the class, this solution allows the problems to recede, making class less stressful for both students and teacher.

Once the problem's impact on education is resolved—not necessarily the problem itself—learning can germinate and thrive. With this in mind, here are some pointers that will help you to support your students:

- Notice your students' needs
- Provide assistance where appropriate
- Promote camaraderie among your students
- Acknowledge progress and honor excellence

Supportive and validating at once, these suggestions help to alleviate the stranglehold that negative outside influences can on students' ability to succeed academically. Your intervention or assistance, even on a small scale, can produce significant benefits for your students.

NOTICE YOUR STUDENTS' NEEDS

Kate's students had needs that were so evident—and in some instances, so disruptive—that they couldn't be overlooked. Identifying such problems is easy; they are literally in your face. However, this is not always the case, particularly when identifying academic needs. Such needs may go unnoticed for various reasons, including:

- The student has become quite proficient at hiding the deficits from adults.
- The student doesn't want to call classmates' attention to their learning needs by seeking the teacher's help.
- Genuine need or deficiency is sometimes mistaken for apathy.

Regardless of the reason that the need is not discovered initially, it's important for the teacher to be on guard for these situations. In fact, students' achievement can hinge on the ability of a teacher to note and then take steps to ameliorate an academic difficulty.

Likewise, disruptive behavioral issues that arise in class occur for various reasons as well, not all of which are simply the students' lack of self-control. Moreover, to assume that the outside issues underlying students' problems can simply be dismissed upon arrival at school is rather dismissive of the students. Instead, consider the following:

- Sometimes a student's unacceptable behavior is an attempt to camouflage academic difficulties. By making jokes, putting forth a running commentary or other distracting behaviors, the student hopes to divert both the teacher's and other students' attention from his or her inability to keep up with the content.
- Alternatively, some students use negative conduct as a means of gaining attention from the teacher or adulation from peers. While drawing negative attention frequently induces negative consequences, for some students, any attention is preferable to none. Furthermore, their willingness to incur the teacher's wrath can prompt sufficient peer approval to make the behavior worth repeating.
- Disruptive behavior is sometimes a reaction to personal issues. While a teacher cannot intervene in domestic affairs, providing students an outlet to express concerns, either with the teacher or with a counselor, can make a tremendous difference in the students' ability to cope with home situations and to adjust their classroom behavior.
- Occasionally, inappropriate behavior indicates a problem beyond the student's control and the teacher's expertise. Requiring additional evaluation, such behaviors then may be deemed in need of special education services. While the upsurge in diagnoses of Attention Deficit Disorder (ADD) and Attention Deficit Hyperactivity Disorder (ADHD), for example, has caused some to conclude that there is overdiagnosis of these conditions, genuine instances of these disorders exist. Nevertheless, these are only two among many diagnoses that may be determined by further evaluation.

It's particularly helpful for students to have behavioral issues addressed not only for their own good but for that of the other students as well, as the behavior can impede the education of everyone in the class. This is another reason that the wise teacher intercedes.

Whether academic or behavioral, addressing students' needs makes learning far more appealing to these students, as it becomes easier for them to meet the challenge. Moreover, the accompanying boost to their academic progress will make your class memorable for years to come as the place where they finally had the breakthrough, with the teacher who cared enough to support students' needs.

PROVIDE ASSISTANCE WHERE APPROPRIATE

Although you teach an entire class, individual students make up this whole. However, for both new and experienced teachers, finding a way to meet students' disparate individual needs in the context of a class period in which delivering content is by necessity the overriding concern can leave a teacher feeling overwhelmed. And "ignore it and it will go away" is not an option, so you must take action.

The good news is that not every need requires your direct assistance; sometimes merely your intervention can resolve the matter. To distinguish between the two, consider the following examples that require only your intervention:

- A "study buddy" or peer helper can offer immeasurable assistance to a student who needs reinforcement of a lesson's main concepts. Working in pairs, a more proficient student who is willing to offer assistance might go over each lesson for a few minutes daily. This provides necessary reinforcement while effectively removing the stigma of having to stay after class with the teacher. Arranging to meet at lunchtime or in your classroom before or after school—rather than during class time—the pair avoids calling class attention to their partnership, and by extension, to the student's need for help. As an incentive to the helper, you might award bonus points or some other academic acknowledgment.
- A student who uses "class clown" antics simply to garner attention might be redirected first by giving him a seat in the front, near the teacher. This effectively thwarts his attempts to have everyone turn toward him. However, if the student's purpose for the behavior is to divert attention from feelings of inadequacy in mastering the content, your direct assistance is needed, and we'll focus on this shortly.
- Students who disrupt class by calling out, offering negative remarks and other behaviors designed to interrupt teaching often are tempered by clearly delineated rules with strong and immediate consequences. While this method may take time, it not only works, it also serves as a deterrent to other students who might be contemplating similar behavior.
- For students whose academic difficulties indicate problems beyond mere comprehension, assistance may take the form of outside intervention. As mentioned earlier for behavioral issues, such instances in the academic arena also might warrant further evaluation. Discussing the students' difficulties with a school guidance counselor, educational evaluator or other professional resource may result in special services being offered to the student.

Highlighting just a few scenarios in which teacher intervention is beneficial, these examples also underscore the importance of early intervention.
Likewise, instances that require direct assistance from the teacher also call
for prompt attention, thereby decreasing the likelihood that the problem will
have a serious impact on students' learning.

Among the situations that might prompt you to take note are:

- Frequent absences could signal a problem. If a student is absent more than
  two consecutive days, you might want to call or e-mail the parent to find
  out the cause and then offer appropriate assistance, if needed. Arranging
  home instruction, for instance, might be necessary for a student with a
  chronic illness. A student burdened with adult responsibilities such as car-
  ing for siblings, translating on behalf of a parent or other concerns might
  need to have the parents apprised of laws concerning attendance. On the
  other hand, if the student is simply skipping class, your query immediately
  apprises parents of the situation.
- Struggling students may need extra help. In conjunction with the "study
  buddy" suggestion offered earlier, some students may require additional help
  from the teacher. By tutoring in your subject for 15 or 20 minutes at the beginning or end of the day, even on a weekly basis, you provide the small setting
  and individual attention that enables some struggling students to catch up.
- A little more praise and fewer reprimands may be the answer for disruptive students. Rather than repeatedly correcting their aberrant behaviors,
  try commending their appropriate behaviors. You might be pleasantly surprised to discover the positive change that sincere compliments and praise
  can produce. The likely result is a reduction in the instances of inappropriate behaviors as students seek to win your praise.

The point here is to note areas where students' independent efforts are
insufficient for their needs or are an obstacle to their own education or that
of others. A teacher's intervention or assistance can have an immensely positive impact. Moreover, the difference this will make in students' achievement
and in their appreciation of learning is invaluable. Ultimately, whatever will
encourage students' academic growth, remove educational impediments or
facilitate learning is worth your effort.

PROMOTE CAMARADERIE AMONG STUDENTS

While a teacher's aid can be essential in resolving student problems, students'
support of one another is an enormous advantage in this area. More than
anything else, adolescents want to be accepted in their peer group, so much

so that peer approval often displaces the parental approval they so ardently sought just a few years earlier. Therefore, by fostering a spirit of camaraderie among students, teachers can channel that desire for peer affirmation into creating a classroom culture that is more conducive to learning. The benefits of encouraging a good rapport among students include:

- Students are more relaxed. As students come to know one another individually, apprehensions and anxieties lessen. Thus, a classroom atmosphere now exists for students to feel safer in asking questions and seeking needed help. Furthermore, it's just easier to learn in a peaceful environment.
- Students are less contentious. Getting along with one another defuses the type of tensions and animosities that Kate contended with in her third period class in the scenario opening this chapter. Students are not quick to relinquish the good will built between them and their classmates to ridicule one another or otherwise create a hostile atmosphere. As a result, student conflicts decrease.
- Students who fit in behave better. Some of the aberrant behaviors of this age group are simply in response to students' perceived feelings of being a misfit. By promoting this esprit de corps, you remove many preconceived social barriers, which in turn, remove a basis for acting-out behaviors.
- Peer pressure maintains classroom order. Equitably enforced, respected rules provide the setting for the lively activities students enjoy, compelling the students to become the guardians of the rules. When a student appears to be a threat to this classroom order, and by extension, to these activities, other students are apt to reinforce the rules by pressuring the disruptive student to conform.
- Students who have come to appreciate each other—differences and all—are more likely to help each other as well. When looking for the aforementioned "study buddy" or other peer helper, your cause is supported by having encouraged mutual respect and understanding between and among your students.
- Students become less judgmental. Becoming familiar with their classmates, students discover that preconceived notions based on subgroup membership don't always fit. As a result, social discourse gets a boost as students look beyond stereotypical identifiers and simply interact.

Given the argument for the advantages of promoting camaraderie among your students, let's turn to a few methods for achieving this. Seemingly simplistic, these steps will develop understanding and respect among your students and may even advance friendships:

- Begin the semester or school year with a bonding or "getting acquainted" activity. An easy idea, this allows students to gain a little knowledge about everyone in the class quickly, in a playful and relaxed manner. The "name game," for example, requires each class member to state his or her first name along with a descriptive adjective beginning with the same letter as the first name. Each subsequent student must remember all preceding names and accompanying adjectives. Another icebreaker pairs students, allotting three minutes to answer autobiographical questions that you have already written on the board. The partner must then introduce the student to the class.

- Incorporate paired activities into your lesson plans. Suggested in chapter two, pairing students for activities has clear educational advantages already explained here. However, the added advantage in this context is that the partners make a mutual investment in the outcome of the endeavor. Working together to achieve a favorable outcome, each must work hard and work well.
- Small-group activities are an additional bond builder. Once again, the exigencies of group work, like paired activities, make it necessary for each member to cooperate. Moreover, learning one another's strengths enables them to assign tasks efficiently and develops appreciation for each member's talents.
- At the midpoint of the semester or school year, try an additional bonding activity. For many, something as common as "Secret Santa" is the perfect midyear activity, further uniting students as each draws a name and secretly purchases a gift for that student. In a twist on this practice, "Nice Week" works beautifully. After drawing names, students spend a week doing an anonymous nice deed for the recipient each day. Anything from a complimentary note to homemade cookies to a dollar-store trinket will work, as kindness, not cost, is the goal. The teacher will need to deliver the items to maintain students' anonymity; however, doing so takes only about five minutes of class time. The overall unity, along with the rapport between the pairs, is priceless.

If you doubt the worth of these activities, experiment first by implementing only one of them. Then watch the result. Or you might conduct all of these activities in only one class. Then compare the unity (or lack thereof) with that of your other classes. You are likely to find that your students in the experimental class have developed bonds that genuinely promote education. Of course, the bonus is that they're enjoying it.

ACKNOWLEDGE PROGRESS, HONOR EXCELLENCE

Everyone enjoys witnessing excellence. From sporting events to award shows to graduation ceremonies, appreciative crowds bestow well-deserved accolades, applause and even trophies on those who demonstrate superior accomplishment. And this appreciation of excellence is just as evident in school, as high-achieving students, lauded with honor awards and scholarships, receive the praise of teachers and the respect of classmates. In view of the high degree of effort required to attain this academic prowess, they warrant all the attention they receive.

However, less stellar students who, nevertheless, have progressively improved over time frequently are ignored. There's no applause and often no acknowledgment of any kind for the student whose grades, for example, rise from C to B. This is not to say that teachers should adopt the popular practice of awarding trophies to everyone who participates; this diminishes genuine accomplishment. Yet, student improvement does merit at least a modicum of recognition.

Some teachers are unwilling to heap what they consider false praise on students, as they deem progress not fundamentally noteworthy. They fear that acknowledgment is to equate improvement with genuine excellence. Yet, it's important to commend progress in your students just as much—but not necessarily in the same manner—as you honor excellence. If unconvinced, here are some reasons to reconsider your mindset:

- Recognizing progress often begets more progress. Students feel encouraged by the acknowledgment of their efforts and, therefore, continue or increase those efforts. The result is even higher levels of achievement.
- A sense of accomplishment becomes an incentive for other endeavors. Receiving a bit of recognition, students use their newly bolstered confidence to attempt other undertakings. This is particularly true for students experiencing a small level of success for the first time, as they now realize that a modicum of success is within their control.
- Affirming students' efforts has a positive effect on their behavior. The rise in self-esteem that ensues from a teacher's recognition can be just what a student needs to transform antagonistic attitudes and disruptive behaviors.

However, being cognizant of the positive effects your recognition can have on your students doesn't always translate into knowing how to offer the most effective recognition. After all, receiving effusive praise for small improvements, students see it for exactly what it is: insincere flattery. No one appreciates that. Instead, consider some of the following acknowledgments:

- Create merit awards. Designed to recognize highly improved students whose grades don't meet honor roll standards, you might award these certificates to students in each of your classes whose grades rise by a predetermined percentage, thereby offering recognition of superior progress.

- Devise an honor award for your subject. Given to the student—or perhaps two students, male and female—whose grades are highest in each of your classes, this award recognizes subject-specific excellence without requiring a high grade point average in all subjects, as is usually stipulated for honor roll students.
- Designate a "Wall of Fame" in your classroom where you display photos of your high-achieving students. Whether you choose to photograph only those with the highest grades in your class or also to include those whose grades have improved significantly, this wall, appropriately labeled, acknowledges academic accomplishment. Be sure to update the photos after each distribution of report cards.
- Collate and display honor roll lists comprised solely of students in your classes. Many schools generate a list of honor roll students and then forward the list to teachers. On receipt of this list, search for names of your students. Then compile honor roll lists of only your students, by class period. When displayed prominently in your classroom, these lists imbue a sense of pride in the honored students and are aspirational for other students.

By whatever method you devise for honoring student achievement, be sure to distinguish between improvement and outstanding accomplishment. Equally deserving of recognition, each also warrants different types of affirmation. These small acknowledgments convey sincere support for your students' accomplishments. Acknowledge progress and honor excellence.

Employing all these tips—from intervention to direct assistance to praise—offers your students humanity. No longer just a face in the crowd, students realize that you see them as worthy of individual attention and support. For some students, your willingness to find personal solutions alters their self-image in a positive way, and with it, their behavior.

All of this, simply because you chose to personalize your approach, seeking ways to overcome the hindrances to students' learning—it's amazing what a little differentiation can do! An unforgettable experience for the students involved, this type of reform really does make students want to be in your class.

Chapter Eight: Support Your Students   **Worksheet**

1. What are the most pressing academic needs among my current students?

_____

_____

_____

_____

_____

_____

_____

_____

_____

_____

_____

2. What specific steps will I take to meet these needs?

_____

_____

_____

_____

_____

_____

_____

_____

_____

_____

_____

_____

_____

Chapter Eight: Support Your Students   **Worksheet**

3. What behavioral issues are preventing specific students from learning?

_____

_____

_____

_____

_____

_____

_____

_____

_____

_____

_____

4. What will I do to alleviate these behavioral interferences?

_____

_____

_____

_____

_____

_____

_____

_____

_____

_____

_____

_____

Chapter Eight: Support Your Students   **Worksheet**

5. What do I currently do to foster camaraderie among my students?

_____

_____

_____

_____

_____

_____

_____

_____

_____

_____

_____

_____

6. How might I enhance student relationships to promote learning?

_____

_____

_____

_____

_____

_____

_____

_____

_____

_____

_____

_____

Chapter Eight: Support Your Students   **Worksheet**

7. What is my philosophy on recognition of student improvement?

_____

_____

_____

_____

_____

_____

_____

_____

_____

_____

_____

_____

8. How might I find ways to acknowledge student progress and honor excellence?

_____

_____

_____

_____

_____

_____

_____

_____

_____

_____

_____

Chapter Eight: Support Your Students **Worksheet**

9. What other suggestions in this chapter will I employ in my classroom?

_____

_____

_____

_____

_____

_____

_____

_____

_____

_____

_____

10. What was the result of my implementation of these suggestions?

_____

_____

_____

_____

_____

_____

_____

_____

_____

_____

_____

Chapter 9

Have Fun!

Mike caught snippets of vibrant conversation—and sometimes, heated debate—as he moved among the small discussion groups formed by his students. Definitely not a calm, quiet atmosphere, a buzz of activity and excited cries of emotion filled the air in his classroom. And this was exactly the way Mike liked it.

His economics students were deeply involved in a cross-discipline project that entailed an environmental impact study, and they were taking the matter quite seriously. Hence, the unabashed displays of fervent opinions comingled with shouts of excitement. And Mike had to admit that he felt deep satisfaction in seeing how far they had come in just a few short months.

Initially, most of the students in his class were rather uncommunicative in response to questions Mike posed or any attempts he made to engage their interests. At the time, discussions and group activities weren't part of his lessons and he hadn't really given much thought to including them. But he also didn't want his students to be as disengaged from his lectures and, by extension, his course, as they seemed to be. So, Mike sought help.

A friend, Brad, who also taught social studies, always seemed to be planning something interesting for his classes. When Mike consulted him, Brad suggested that Mike spice up his lectures with less emphasis on lecturing and more focus on meaningful student interaction. Brad lent him a couple of resource books and also invited Mike to accompany him to an upcoming social studies conference.

At the conference, Mike attended a break-out session on innovative teaching practices and learned tips for working with students in small groups. In addition, he received helpful resource materials that he could use with his students as well as information on a couple of professional organizations, one of which he later joined. This organization provided exactly the sort of collegiality Mike needed along with some great suggestions and ideas that he began using in his lessons.

Brad also agreed to sit in on Mike's class and to give him some pointers on ways to elicit greater participation and enthusiasm from his students. What's more, Brad allowed Mike to observe him and glean whatever might be helpful from his observations.

All of this paid off as Mike's teaching took on a different, livelier tone and so did the atmosphere in his classroom. Now, Mike found that he derived a great deal of pleasure from planning a successful lesson. And he defined his success by his student's willingness to participate in it as well as from the information they retained from it.

Gone were the deadpan gazes and silent stares in response to lectures. Instead, Mike's students were now involved in learning that kindled their interest. And as they gradually learned new concepts, they enjoyed applying them in new ways, such as the economics project they were currently doing.

Both teaching and learning had become enjoyable. And Mike had become a teacher whose students now wanted to be in his class—actually, so did a few of their friends.

RISING FROM MEDIOCRE TO SUPERB

Mike is an education reformer. Not satisfied to accept mediocrity, he wanted a more invigorating educational experience for his students—one that transcended test scores to promote genuine learning. Now, great things are going on in his classroom: vigorous discussions, participatory learning, a teacher who is a catalyst for learning rather than the focus of it, and . . . an overall good time. Clearly, Mike has created a very successful educational environment. And it all occurred because he learned to reform the education that was taking place in his classroom so that it met the needs of his students. That's real education reform.

And that's the point here: to determine what's going well and distinguish it from what needs tweaking and from what should be relinquished in order to create the learning environment that produces successful students. Just as Mike did, you can revolutionize your classroom and forever alter the way your students perceive education in three simple steps:

- Take the time to evaluate your methods of teaching and your students' responses to it.
- Decide what works and retain it.
- Discard or improve the remaining portions of your pedagogy

This is the essence of successful reform. Mike took education a step further by injecting enjoyment into his lessons—for himself and his students. Yes, he wanted his students to be active learners, but he also wanted them to enjoy the process. This factor takes education from acceptable to excellent.

Moreover, Mike wanted to experience the satisfaction inherent in bringing out the best in his students and watching them soar. As a result, his satisfaction level with his job became stratospheric as he achieved these goals.

For students, the excitement is in education that takes them into the realm of relevant learning with real-world connections. Interactions among students, and between students and teacher, create the environment in which education can take root. Along with the liberty to take abstract concepts in a textbook and make them concrete (through their own efforts), learning then becomes real and enjoyable. This is precisely the educational environment Mike provided.

Taking an ordinary—and what might have been acceptable—method of teaching, Mike transformed it into the extraordinary by:

- Realizing there was a need for change
- Seeking help when he could not pinpoint his problem
- Being open to new experiences, including attending a conference and joining a professional organization
- Incorporating what he learned into his teaching
- Redesigning his lessons to make them student-centered rather than teacher-centered
- Soliciting and valuing students' participation

Because of Mike's efforts, active learning combined with engaging activities to produce an energized learning atmosphere. And while you don't need to replicate Mike's classroom, his ability to assess his shortcomings honestly and adapt accordingly is worth emulating. As you reform your methods, incorporating the tools here—and whichever others you choose to include— you take your class from mediocre to superb.

REMEMBER WHY YOU TEACH

While you're working on your personalized reforms, remember to keep your focus on your original purpose—the reasons you became an educator. Maintaining your own foundational principles at the forefront—those intangible, value-laden ideals that propelled you into this profession—undergirds your attempts to energize your teaching and boost your students' learning. Those ideals represent your educational value system and can serve as somewhat of a blueprint for your approach to teaching.

This is why all the advice in the world—including that offered here—is of little merit if it causes you to lose sight of the standards and beliefs that are intrinsic to your personal ideology regarding education and your role in it. These values are the reasons you continue to teach today. Or, if you are just beginning, they are what induced you to enter this vocation.

Common among these ideals for many educators are:

- Your personal respect for education
- Your desire to make a definitive educational difference
- Your enjoyment of the subject(s) you teach
- Your interest in sharing that same pleasure in the subject with your students
- Your wish to have a positive impact, educationally and personally on today's youth

Your reasons for being an educator may encompass these or not, but they will encourage you to continue on the days when your noble goals seem remote and will buoy you higher on the days when everything is splendid. Moreover, they bolster your sense of accomplishment in a job well done as you see your ideals come to fruition in your students' sustained academic achievement.

ENJOY YOURSELF

Since education and the reform of it need not be onerous tasks, to put it simply, enjoy what you do. Mike's sense of fulfillment was immense as he observed his students' boisterous, yet purposeful, interactions. In addition to taking pride in watching measurable academic growth over such a brief period, their ability to infuse serious educational undertakings with their own enthusiasm and interest made Mike's job that much more rewarding. That's a great bonus!

In fact, with all the emphasis in this book on techniques and tips to make your class more appealing to your students, none of this would be worth doing if it were not also enjoyable to you. And if that sounds odd, you may have missed the point of this book. Gratuitous merriment is not important, but rather engaging activities that support and sustain students' educational interest and your educational objectives.

Therefore, to ensure your own enjoyment of this profession, be sure that you:

- Derive as much gratification from the lessons you prepare as your students obtain from learning them.
- Make sure that the enhancements and novelty you introduce to your students heighten the educational interest for you as well.
- Remember to keep your eye on the joy of it all as you change, adapt, adjust, and discard methodologies to develop lessons with your imprimatur.

Students and teachers deserve to benefit equally from the education process and from any changes you choose to implement. The education profession—in which paperwork and perpetual testing can feel burdensome—offers its practitioners endless possibilities for making education at once meaningful and enjoyable. And if you're not having fun with your lessons, how will your students ever know that the subject you teach can be enjoyable? How will they ascertain that learning can be exciting? By demonstrating this, you leave a lasting imprint on their lives.

LEAVE YOUR IMPRINT

Once your students discover how enticing learning can be, they can take this discovery with them into other academic arenas. This is your educational legacy, so to speak, your imprint on their lives and on their education. And years from now, although your students may not recall every detail of the facts you've taught them, they will remember *how* you taught them: with vigor, enthusiasm, confidence in their ability to grasp the concepts and go forth with them, engendering a desire to know more.

Mike's students are not likely to forget the educational imprint he has made on them. Providing information and then encouragement, he compelled them to analyze, evaluate and synthesize knowledge as a means of learning. Having built their critical-thinking skills, his students now own that knowledge. And Mike's role in their education is apt to have a significant influence on his students' learning for years to come. This is his legacy, the imprint he has made on their educational lives.

Of course, the goal here is that your impact be positive and enduring. This ability to leave a positive legacy for students is derived from several factors:

- Your understanding of students' educational needs and seeking to meet them
- Your ability—indeed, your power—to mold your students' educational destiny simply by the way you impart knowledge

- Your willingness to put forth the full effort needed to ensure their academic achievement
- The authority of your position to empower students to become lifelong learners who approach learning opportunities eagerly or perpetual shirkers who shy away from anything vaguely reminiscent of education

These enduring qualities leave an equally durable imprint on your students' lives, unlike that of any other profession. Exercise this power with reverence and care so that your imprint is both valued and valuable.

LEARN FROM MISTAKES AND KEEP GROWING

Gained only through experience, your unique brand of educational excellence is not fully crafted at the start of your teaching career, despite the best training, but rather is an ongoing process. Therefore, if you are a new teacher, know that you will make mistakes, have difficult days, and sometimes frustration will mount. Expect this. What's important is that you use your mistakes and difficulties as opportunities to learn, to improve, to innovate. As an educator, your need for continued professional growth is paramount.

Veterans of the profession, on the other hand, find the biggest obstacle is often stagnation, an insidious foe. The best advice in such instances is to fight it assiduously. For just as the new teacher is often surprised, and even disillusioned, facing the intricacies of teaching that simply were not covered in college classes, veteran educators often are equally nonplussed to find that they must continue to change, adapt, and progress to avoid complacency and, even worse, obsolescence. The ability and willingness to make these adjustments empowers you as you refine your craft and move increasingly closer to being the kind of teacher that you hoped to be when you first began.

Despite all the newfangled proposals and much-hyped reforms presented by "experts"—who more often than not are outside the field of education, but who nonetheless purport to have the answers to today's education crises— real education reform begins with you, the classroom teacher. Beyond standardized test scores, the most rewarding measure of your success—and of your legacy and imprint—will be reflected in the student who has heard about your classroom methods and asks, "Can I be in your class?"

Hearing that question from a student who is eager to learn, you'll know that you're succeeding, that you have already made a great impact on your students' educational lives. That's education reform.

Chapter Nine: Have Fun!   **Worksheet**

1. What specific steps can I take to transform my teaching methods from mediocre to superb?

    _____

    _____

    _____

    _____

    _____

    _____

    _____

    _____

    _____

    _____

    _____

2. What are my educational values and ideals that will support me on difficult teaching days?

    _____

    _____

    _____

    _____

    _____

    _____

    _____

    _____

    _____

    _____

    _____

Chapter Nine: Have Fun!   **Worksheet**

3. What do I most enjoy about teaching?

_____

_____

_____

_____

_____

_____

_____

_____

_____

_____

_____

_____

4. What can I change or eliminate to make teaching more enjoyable for me?

_____

_____

_____

_____

_____

_____

_____

_____

_____

_____

_____

_____

Chapter Nine: Have Fun! **Worksheet**

5. How can I help my students desire to be lifelong learners?

_____

_____

_____

_____

_____

_____

_____

_____

_____

_____

_____

_____

6. What mistakes have I learned from as a teacher?

_____

_____

_____

_____

_____

_____

_____

_____

_____

_____

_____

_____

_____

_____

Chapter Nine: Have Fun!   **Worksheet**

7. What do I need to do to become the teacher I always wanted to be?

_____

_____

_____

_____

_____

_____

_____

_____

_____

_____

_____

_____

8. What educational legacy do I want to leave my students?

_____

_____

_____

_____

_____

_____

_____

_____

_____

_____

_____

_____

Chapter Nine: Have Fun! **Worksheet**

9. What other suggestions in this chapter will I employ in my classroom?

_____

_____

_____

_____

_____

_____

_____

_____

_____

_____

_____

_____

10. What was the result of my implementation of these suggestions?

_____

_____

_____

_____

_____

_____

_____

_____

_____

_____

_____

_____

Index

About the Author

Denise Fawcett Facey is the author of *The Social Studies Helper: Creative Assignments for Exam Success.* An award-winning educator, she is a national and local conference speaker and conducts workshops training teachers to understand and reach the diverse students of the twenty-first-century classroom.

Made in the USA
Columbia, SC
14 March 2025

55141314R00078